Matthew Hardy is a comedian who was the writer for the ABC's *The Fat*, is currently a writer for TEN's BAFTA Award-winning *The Sketch Show* and appeared on Triple M before joining Melbourne sports radio SEN drive time program *The Run Home*, with Dermott Brereton and Anthony Hudson. He wrote for Greg Champion of ABC Radio's *Coodabeens* before becoming a regular performer at The Comedy Store in London, returning to Australia for the Melbourne Comedy Festival, where he performed a one-man show of his bestselling book, *Saturday Afternoon Fever*, to rave reviews.

Praise for *Saturday Afternoon Fever*

'The funniest book I have ever read in my entire life. I must have read it ten times and have woken my wife by laughing too loud on more than one occasion.' – Garry Lyon, quoted in *Women's Weekly*

'It's not often a book makes me laugh out loud but this one did. I was hooked from the opening page. Hardy is to be applauded for this heart-breaking and exciting tale of his teenage years. Enjoy the ride as Hardy portrays a time when all that mattered was having as much fun as you could with your mates.' – Jamie Tate, *Herald-Sun*

'A suburban boy with suburban neuroses and suburban charm, Hardy writes with humour, self-deprecation and insight. His description of the first time he has sex is, at times, painfully funny. Among the high farce of his life, Hardy pulls off some poignant moments. It's autobiography, yet it would also sit well as anthropology. A fascinating study of a man's mind.' – Peter Lalor, *The Daily Telegraph*

'Absolutely loved it. A beautiful story. Full of heart and magical memories.' – Michelle Van Ray, MIX FM

'Shitloads of laughs . . . highly recommended. Look out for the reference to Caramello Koala. Unfortunately, I lent my copy to my brother, who lent it to his mate Bulldog, who can't remember who he lent it to. Any chance of another one?' – Merrick & Rosso

'Whichever page I opened the book at, there was something funny straight away. The bit about Hardy's strange connection with '70s Carlton star Vinnie Cattoggio is my favourite. Sensational!' – Mark Harvey, Essendon Football Club legend

'Awesome!' – Dwayne Russell, 3AW and Channel Nine

'This is a great book. I laughed my arse off!' – Liz Ellis, Australian Netball Captain

'Most men will see a little bit of themselves in *Saturday Afternoon Fever.* No doubt our wives and girlfriends would claim to see a whole lot more.' – Russell Holmesby, *Inside Football*

'Laugh-out-loud funny, but if you didn't laugh you'd cry. Even if you hate football you might enjoy this book. Honest, entertaining, insightful and poignant.' – Peter Ascot, *Big Issue*

'Matthew Hardy is a very special talent, which this great book confirms.' – Bert Newton, *Good Morning Australia*

SATURDAY AFTERNOON FEVER

A FOOTY FAN'S MEMOIR OF A LIFE ON THE OUTER LOOKING IN

MATTHEW HARDY

RANDOM HOUSE AUSTRALIA

Random House Australia Pty Ltd
Level 3, 100 Pacific Highway, North Sydney, NSW 2060
http://www.randomhouse.com.au

Sydney New York Toronto
London Auckland Johannesburg

First published in Australia by HarperCollinsPublishers
Pty Limited 1999, 2002
First published by Random House Australia 2004

National Library of Australia
Cataloguing-in-Publication Entry

Hardy, Matthew, 1969-.
Saturday afternoon fever.

ISBN 1 74051 350 9.
ISBN 978 1 74051 350 0.

1. Football fans – Victoria – Biography. 2. Australian football – Victoria. I. Title.

6.336

Cover image by GAP Media
Cover design by Jason Hynes, and Darian Causby/Highway 51
Printed and bound by Griffin Press

for Mum and Dad

Acknowledgments

Australia:

All family, all friends, Russell Gilbert, Greg Champion, Barry Dickins, Dave O'Neil, Virginia Dunlevie, Bert Newton, Tatia Sloley plus King at Associates, Andrew and Kate at Access Comedy, Michael Lynch and Trevor Marmalade. And, especially, Garry Lyon and all at radio SEN. Thanks to Luke Hardy for the cover image and hello to Jake, Scott and Caroline.

England:

All family, all friends, Gin and the Clarke clan, Malcolm and Jane Hardee, Jim and Alison Tavare, Mark Wells, Julia Lindsay, Paul Tonkinson, Duddridge Management, Avalon, Terry Alderton and the amazing Leena Similu.

Book:

Fran Bryson and Lucy Williams at AMC. Alison Urquhart especially, Jesse Fink, Sarah Gentle and all at HarperCollins. Saint Kilda Football Club, Peter Lyssiotis and The Brotherhood. Ed Byrne, Michael Nevinson, Skepper and Gympus.

Contents

CHAPTER ONE

The Beginning

I discovered passion in a packet of footy cards. They were all the rage, and I wanted in on the action. Opening my very first set of six cards with the chewy on top, I was greeted by the sight of Trevor Barker's long blond locks. He seemed part Hollywood movie star, part comic-book superhero, and instantly, I wanted to know more about him. Anyone or anything able to create such an adrenaline rush was worth investigating.

A quick shuffle through the other five footy cards offered Barker no competitor when it came to charisma: a Fitzroy forward named, amusingly I thought, Bob Beecroft; Hawthorn ruckman Don Scott (wearing a skivvy!); two Collingwood players, whom I ignored through what must have been instinct; a Footscray checklist; and Rex Hunt, also in St Kilda colours yet more memorable for his photographic resemblance to Bugs Bunny. No, it had to be Barker.

Whatever kind of man I have become since then is the direct result of walking into my local milk bar some time during the 1978 footy season, aged nine, and walking out into a whole new world. Like my first successful swim without Floaties, this act miraculously altered my life forever. Barker had become the alchemist of my ambition. Unlike most of my mates, I'd not harboured any dreams of becoming an astronaut or a fire-fighter. Now, there could be no doubt of my future. I wasn't just going to be a footballer. I wanted to be Trevor Barker. From that moment, I could think of nothing else. His face on that footy card, like a lily on a pond, remained floating on the surface of my mind. Twenty years later, it still does.

I'd decided to barrack for St Kilda earlier on. Their motif matched the one on my favourite toy, a Matchbox model of Simon Templar's white Jaguar from the TV series *Return of the Saint*. Barracking meant replying 'St Kilda' whenever anyone asked which team I supported, but that was as far as it went. I knew nothing at all about the club — or the game itself, for that matter.

Scanlen's footy cards had a smell all their own. The flat slice of chewing gum tasted better than other types and gave out a fruity sort of scent. It was covered in a sugary white powder, which I liked blowing off the first card once the perfectly folded waxed-paper wrapping was removed. I'd then wipe the card down with my shirtsleeve, to find it in mint condition. The powder enhanced the card's sheen, like breath on glass.

Card-swapping was frustrating. In the space of a few weeks, I'd gone from wondering what all the fuss was about among the kids crowding noisily around the taps at playtime to being an all-knowing obsessive. 'Got, got, got, haven't ...' barked the buyers as the salesmen flicked through their available goods. Not many collectors looked after their cards the way I did. Some claimed to have a card I wanted, only to produce one that was dog-eared or had cut edges from a rubber band too tightly wrapped.

'Alle de Wolde is worth his weight in gold', we said at the shelter-shed swap market. The Hawk defender was 'rare' when it came to collecting. I doubt the company printed fewer of a particular player simply to keep us keen. Everyone had their own idea about who was hard to get hold of. Some players did appear to be mass-produced. One year there was a flood of Simon Maddens, and the season I started, Richmond's Bob Heard reached plague proportions. The cards were our form of currency. A good bargain lifted my mood for months.

Some swappers showed such limited knowledge, I lost respect for them. They were kids who collected to be a part of the crowd, operating with an obvious lack of passion. Receiving a rare Alle de Wolde in return for a surplus Simon Madden made me happy on one hand, yet upset me on the other, purely because they weren't playing properly. Just as Eric Idle's street merchant in Monty Python's *Life Of Brian* didn't want anyone to buy without bartering, even if they offered him an excellent price, I too enjoyed the art of the deal.

On the back of each of the three hundred available footy cards was a little part of what became a large picture. It was a puzzle that added up to a poster-sized portrait of some star taking a screamer. The idea didn't interest me. I was a lot older before I learned that patience has its own rewards.

Financing my fixation was a problem until Grandpa devised a plan: twenty cents to buy a packet each time I did the dishes. This motivation gave me wrinkly fingers for a full season. Like Madge from the TV commercial, I was soaking in green dishwashing liquid every second hour, the constant exposure literally giving me olive palms, so its name was appropriate.

Carlton rover Vinnie Catoggio's card was a personal favourite, because I thought his name sounded sensational. Wrapping my lips around the pronunciation was a physical pleasure: Ca-todg-ee-yo. Vinnie wore the most outrageous afro anyone had ever seen. If he wasn't old, white and unattractive, he might have been mistaken for a member of The Jackson Five.

One of the many unbreakable code rules among my mates was to say 'Vince' following a fart. This served as both a proud announcement of the event and a warning of the approaching aroma. The origins of 'Vince' remain unknown, but it had been around for years. After the footy card was issued, it was adjusted to 'Vince Catoggio', before eventually evolving to a simple 'Catoggio'. I bet Vinnie would rather his name be remembered for his fine footy skills than used as a warning that someone just farted!

St Kilda often signed players from other teams after the season's cards had been printed. Their image seemed strange in another team's jumper when I was watching them wear ours each week, so I solved the dilemma with photo-fits. I'd cut the face of, say, Max Crow, who arrived from Essendon, off his Bomber-clad torso, then paste it over a spare Saint. Thus I'd create a unique new card and keep my collection up-to-date. It was an inspired idea. More practical than anything I'd seen on *The Curiosity Show*.

Card design varied each season. One set printed the players' on-field positions. St Kilda's Glenn Elliot played as a 'utility'. Where? I'm sure Scanlen's invented that one themselves. No doubt it was a reference to the trusty 'ute' — able to do any job.

I began collecting around the time Scanlen's opted to go for head-and-shoulder shots. Previously, players had been photographed pretending to handpass, poised to drop the ball onto their boot, or scooping it, one-handed, off the grass, all whilst smiling for the camera. Surely not a smart way to prepare for potential shirtfrontery. My footy card fever ceased some seasons on, when Scanlen's again decided to portray the stars 'in action', this time using snapshots taken during matches. This scenario was unsatisfying, allowing some players to be pictured completely out of character — a forward shown going the punch from behind, for example, or Kevin 'Hungry' Bartlett passing to a team-mate in a better position. It wasn't right. In fact, it was downright improper, and time for me to retire.

CHAPTER TWO

The Neighbourhood

Set deep in Melbourne's south-eastern suburbs, our four-bedroom, red-brick house with front and back yards stood out from the rest, because unlike our neighbours' homes, which were all aesthetically aligned parallel to the front fence and, therefore, the road, my parents had requested that their house be built diagonally across the block, in order to avoid the direct sun during the summer.

Dad migrated to Australia from Britain in 1950, taking on a job in the Victorian Police Force. Seven years later, he ended up in Bendigo, rural Victorian home of the 1850s gold rush, where this tall, dark and handsome Englishman was considered quite a catch. My mother caught him. After their marriage, Peter Hardy and Margot Hammil headed for the smoke, initially settling in Ringwood, slightly beyond the suburban outline. Two boys were born there: Mark and Simon. My arrival coincided with a move closer to the GPO, to more spacious surroundings in Glen Waverley.

A thirty-minute drive from Melbourne's city centre, Glen Waverley was an orchard area until absorbed by the urban sprawl. New estates were created, and since then,

Glen Waverley and its original settlers have progressed together. Most of those early inhabitants are still there, living in the homes they built during the late 1960s. Enormous trees that stand now as local landmarks are visible as waist-high saplings in the background of our family photos. I could walk along our street today and still know the surname of almost every family.

If the Cunningham's on *Happy Days* embody the 'apple pie' ideal of mainstream America, then the average Glen Waverley family could well be seen as representing the 'meat pie' ideal of mainstream Australia: neither rich nor poor, two point four kids, car, dog, front lawn. Glen Waverley may well be the modern-day 'suburb's suburb', overtaking Dame Edna's Moonee Ponds as *the* Australian suburban touchstone. Certainly, if the scent of gum leaves burning in a Sunday afternoon incinerator could be bottled, then naming it *eau de glenwav* would not be inappropriate.

The national cultural cringe ensured that all Australians unashamedly lionised anything from overseas, in particular the US and the UK. We had no doubt they were better than us in every aspect, from the arts to agriculture, rarely stopping to wonder why, with our minimal comparative population, we were able to compete with — and beat — any nation in the sporting arena. Even Clancy, the blonde cousin in *Skippy* who stayed at Waratah National Park with the Hammonds for a while, was the show's most intriguing character, purely on account of her English accent.

So ravenous was our appetite for overseas influences in 1978 that those of us living in Melbourne's south-eastern suburbs were honoured when the Seven-Eleven company selected our area in which to open one of its first Australian stores, on the corner of Blackburn and Waverley roads. We felt the world's eyes on us when the big day arrived. No expense was spared. Marching bands and radio personalities mixed happily with the average mums and dads. Surrounding streets were closed for miles around, and people came from far and wide in their best clothes to witness the red ribbon being cut by — wait for it — Caramello Koala. Yep, it was class all the way, with organisers leaving no stone unturned in their efforts to make this an event to remember. Add unlimited free Slurpees for the day and it's easy to see why the package was so attractive to the thousands who revelled in the razzamatazz. It was the most exciting day since Johnny Farnham sang *Sadie, the Cleaning Lady* from the back of the 3XY radio fun-bus in the K-Mart carpark in Burwood. He later chucked prizes into the crowd and Mark caught Ker-Plunk. Glen Waverley may have been a half-hour drive from the GPO, but with major chain-store recognition in the shape of our own Seven-Eleven, there would be no stopping us now.

The area's atmosphere was convivial. Come Christmas time, the postman would leave his motorbike for a minute and step inside for a quick cold can. Each house issued the same invitation. The chosen few he accepted considered themselves 'one up' on those he politely refused. Our neighbourhood cachet was enhanced whenever Stan (for we were familiar!) paused and then said, 'Yeah, why not? It won't do any harm'. How the postie, like Santa himself, managed to continue his work after the first few houses, with their 'glass of beer and a slice of Christmas cake', is a mystery. Stan loved our dog Coco, who was a caramel-coloured hybrid of various breeds, described by Mum as 'bitzer'. Coco had been taught to beg for her dog biscuits. We enjoyed exhibiting this trick for our friends. Balancing on her back legs was the least she could do if it meant gobbling down a Good-O. We'd hold one out in front, at the end of a straight arm until she'd performed the feat, then let it drop into her mouth, saying 'Good Girl' as if we were talking to a baby.

'Lick Your Chops' we said when she'd finished chewing.

Mark took great pleasure in making her balance, back straight, for what must've seemed like hours to the poor mutt, only to open an empty hand at the end of it all. He still said 'Good Girl', just to confuse her.

There was a certain spot on her tummy which, when I tickled it, made her rear left leg kick back and forth at a million miles an hour. There was another bit on her back, above her tail. She licked the air whenever I rubbed it, like she had an invisible lolly-pop in front of her. I feel uneasy in hindsight because although Coco had been spayed, it was probably a rude type of reaction.

The Family

Waving Simon off to England when he went to stay with Grandpa was a major worry, not because I would miss him, though I would, but because we knew Mum would drag us all out onto the Tullamarine viewing ledge to wave at the plane.

Mum had devised a plan for farewelling people at the airport. She would request that the departing friend or family member sit at a window seat (or borrow somebody else's for a minute), then lift the blind up and down three times in a row, to let her know where they were. She would let them know where she was by waving a teatowel, which she never forgot to bring for the ritual. With the plane so far away, the glare factor and the heaving masses alongside us on the viewing ledge, both parts of this plan were almost impossible. Despite regular embarrassed pleas from me for her to desist, and a constant stream of light-hearted derogatory remarks from Dad, Mum stood firm.

In this particular instance, having bade Simon a teary-eyed good-bye, Mum got herself into position and reached into her bag for the teatowel, only to discover it was not there. In the midst of accusing Dad and me (Mark being old enough to totally avoid such a scenario by staying home) of hiding it from her, Mum realised she'd left it on the roof of the car 'for a second' before getting in. Thinking Simon would be disappointed ('More like relieved!' Dad suggested), tears were beginning to well, until she had a brainwave. Off came her windcheater, the pink one with a hand-painted portrait of Coco on the front, and there she stood, clad in her industrial-strength Mum-brand bra, waving the windcheater above her head.

And this was years before Kevin Sheedy began annoying opposition supporters with the same technique. A Japanese man took photos.

When Simon rang to say he'd arrived safely, Mum was upset to find he hadn't been able to see a thing anyway, because of the sun in his eyes. 'More like the shame in his soul', Dad said, dodging an accurately aimed teaspoon.

Mum loved to sing *Up There Cazaly* as she ironed our shirts for school. It was a favourite of ours, too. Whenever our parents were outside, Mark would play the single in the lounge room, throwing Coco high into the air each time the chorus came around. Coco Cazaly! Dogs aren't blessed with the perfect balance of cats, so whenever Coco became airborne, she showed signs of pure panic. There was no need, because Mark always caught her again. I reckon she may even have enjoyed the attention. These were moments of pure pleasure for Simon and me, because with Mark being older and more interested in booze and girls, he was rarely around the house. This way, we could hang out with him, torment the dog and sing footy songs at the same time. Bliss.

To put it in the nicest possible way, Mark was always a bit mental. I suppose part of his duty as first-born was to smooth a path for his siblings to follow. After an argument with Mum or Dad, he'd lock his bedroom door behind him and put *Why Don't You All Get Fucked?* by Skyhooks on his record player, full blast. On his panel van was a bumper-sticker that said 'Tammy Has One — Mal Is One'. While this was purely a statement of his personal political views, quite a few of the neighbours still called by to complain. Mum didn't make much mention of it, because even in her own cleaner vocabulary, she thought much the same about our then Prime Minister. Whenever Malcolm Fraser appeared on the telly, she'd switch channels straight away, saying stuff like, 'What a lot of bloody bullshit', which was as extreme an oath as I ever heard from her. While I didn't know a great deal about the government, I knew Malcolm Fraser followed Carlton and I could therefore well understand Mum's viewpoint.

We used to visit my aunt and uncle at their home in South Melbourne each month before I became a footy fanatic. With its high ceilings, extra-large light switches, and fully functioning cast-iron washing wringer out the back, it felt as if we were stepping back in time. Uncle Tom was a veteran South Melbourne supporter who listened to their games on the radio, an ice-cold bottle of Melbourne Bitter beside him. '3KZ *is* football', crackled Captain Blood and the Major down the corridor. Uncle Tom had a hot-line through to the local SP bookie, and when not studying the pink pages of *The Sporting Globe*, he did those circle-the-word quiz books for relaxation. Saturday afternoon cigars sent him to sleep but not before he'd taken off the paper ring from around the middle for me to wear on the way home.

Auntie Anne and Uncle Tom always came for Christmas dinner, meaning Simon and I had to eat ours at a card table in the lounge room, because there wasn't enough room in the kitchen. It was lonely in there, listening to all the animated conversation in the next room, the two of us in our coloured crêpe-paper 'cracker' hats, reading each other the awful jokes and asking for more stuffing.

Nana lived with us. Mum's mum. She contributed to the mortgage when Mum and Dad were married, in return for her own section of the house. A sliding door at the end of the corridor provided privacy when required. Her slice of the homestead was referred to as 'Nana's End'. Her room had a soft, purple hue. With a large make-up mirror framed in elaborately detailed brass, part of a varnished redwood vanity piece. In front of the mirror lay a silver tray complete with a four piece purple handled hair styling set. Sepia toned framed photographs of my late Grandfather and my mother as a girl (in long braided pigtails) sat on doilies to one side. On the other, a musical jewellery box. Her lounge room featured a photo of an English cottage with a thatched roof where she'd once lived, and a classic Swiss cuckoo clock which I ran down to watch on the hour whenever I remembered. Nana liked to sip the odd sherry on the sly. Mum occasionally joined her for a tipple. We knew what they'd been up to when they began touching their toes. Mark, Simon and I were all unable to touch ours, be it through lack of flexibility, slipped discs or whatever else sounded believable. Having gargled a few glasses, my Mum and her Mum would both start bending down and back up again, endlessly, in a bid to prove their pliability. It was bizarre. Nana was pushing ninety, Mum was pushing fifty and there they were, standing next to each other in the kitchen, arms up in the air like two men on the mark, before touching their toes in tandem. It was actually impressive, even if it looked ridiculous. They'd tell us how hopeless we all were in comparison before getting the giggles and eventually giving up. Whenever we annoyed her, Nana threatened to 'box our ears', a saying which we found funny instead of fearful.

The Good Life

Before football enveloped my every waking hour, I was mad about the drive-in movies. The concept still strikes me as the finest form of entertainment ever invented. It was almost as if a child had conceived a plan to which the adults agreed: outside, yet in the car, staying up late while watching a movie, with popcorn for sale, and swings to play on before the whole thing started! Though we didn't go as often as I'd have liked, the times we spent parked on the open lot in Oakleigh with the heavyweight speaker hooked inside the wound-up window rank among the most magical of my childhood.

The Oxford English dictionary defines the word 'fantastic' as 'extravagantly fanciful, extraordinary'. Our inaugural trip to the drive-in was just that. We watched *Herbie Goes Bananas*, or so Mum thought. Truth be told, we spent our time in the back seat trying to see the gigantic pair of boobs behind us on the second screen. To scale, they were probably of standard size, but spread across forty feet, those massive bare breasts made the idea of a flying Volkswagen seem sensible.

It might have been *Last Tango In Paris* which had me popping out of my pyjamas and looking for a blanket to lay across my little lap. All the while sucking on my Kool-Mints in a slobbering state of excitement.

Straight out of the Sunday bath, Mum ironed our 'jarmies just before she handed them over, so they'd still be nice and warm when we slipped them on. Simon and I vied for pole position in front of the Vulcan gas heater, trying not to burn our bare bums on the hot glass while we waited.

'Here you are' Mum said as she passed the PJs, 'You better put them on quick. There's a birdie outside looking for a worm'.

Music was also a big part of our household. Skyhooks were just one of the bands I liked. Their *Living In The Seventies* album was one of Mark's favourites. I liked whatever Mark and Simon played. I had to. They monopolised the stereo and I rarely had any money to buy records anyway. Mark built up an extensive collection, though he preferred Australian outfits such as Dragon, Mother Goose, Cold Chisel and AC/DC. Everything of Mark's was on vinyl, whereas Simon's serious interest in music coincided with cassette tapes, so he favoured the new format. Whilst Mark was mental, Simon was mellow. Simon would occasionally cry when frustrated or depressed, whereas Mark, in the same situation, would put his fist through a wall.

A six-week stay with our Grandfather in England must've had a musical influence, for Simon's collection leaned mainly towards British bands. Status Quo, Queen, ELO and Madness were among his most-played. In our bunk beds (Simon and I shared a room), we'd fall asleep with these sounds on the tape recorder. Mum and Dad had a scattered selection between them. Mum's Abba singles were played to saturation point. She had some good Leo Sayer songs, and Neil Diamond's *Hot August Night* LP was a family favourite. My first single was *Howzat*, by Sherbet, which I bought because I thought it was about cricket. In fact it was a tale of infidelity. I still say it was an understandable mistake. Then Suzie Quatro came along and sent my undies a'quiver. All that leather wrapped around the one lady! Hubba Hubba!! I was a late developer and didn't know much about stiffies, only that Quatro had a lot to do with them.

Skyhooks lead singer was Shirley Strachan. 'Shirl the Curl' as he called himself, hosted the 'Super 66' draw on Saturday nights. If his team, Hawthorn, had won, he'd tell us all about the game in between calling the numbers. He was one of many celebrities I couldn't feel completely comfortable watching because I knew who they barracked for. Molly Meldrum, on the other hand, was a must. Every Sunday night, I'd catch *Countdown*, not so much for the musical offerings as to see if he mentioned the Saints.

The Wheels

The three-speed Malvern Star (complete with specially modified AM/FM radio mounted on the handlebars) expanded my horizons beyond belief. Before the bike, the world was restricted to where I could walk. With my new school, Syndal Tech, only a mile away and my friends within three blocks, there was no need to go anywhere else. I'd not caught a bus further than the train station. Trains were only for finding football grounds with my middle brother, Simon. Then it was off one train and onto another. Exploration hadn't entered my mind.

There were two areas of local wasteland if we wanted adventure. Both could be found on foot. The Red Dam was our outback, a vast region of clay-like dirt with deep ditches and a dam in the middle, where we fished for yabbies in the summer. Then there was our jungle, Valley Reserve, an out-of-control council park with top-secret tracks worn through a wealth of brushwood, where we fished for tadpoles in winter. The benefits of bike ownership were mind-boggling. A twenty-minute walk became a two-minute ride. I travelled the sorts of distances that Dad drove in the car. I set eyes on surrounding suburbs for the first time and thought I had an idea of what Captain Cook must have experienced. As this new world unfolded before me, my options appeared endless.

I had a crush on Kerrie Paddington. She reminded me of Samantha from *Bewitched*. Her house was now within reach. She played hockey for the girls' school side. There were better-looking girls, but none made me so nervous. She lived in a secluded street that wasn't on the way to anywhere. I rode past repeatedly on Sunday afternoons, hoping she might happen to head outside while I was 'in the area'. 'Is this your place?' I planned to ask casually. 'What a coincidence! Wanna dink?' She never did sit on my pack-rack. Hours, days, weeks later, I heard the front door open as I rolled along outside. Could it be? Yes, it is. Here she comes, I confirmed fearfully. My legs peddled me away as far and as fast as they could go. Useless.

Everybody I knew endured a big bike stack, the type that scars for life. My brother Mark once rounded a corner at full pace and ran headlong into a parked car, barely avoiding a broken neck. Simon was sailing down a hill towards a main road, in the rain, when his brakes failed, forcing a desperate detour into a driveway. He 'came to' in a kind lady's lounge room with a slice out of his scalp. My turn came as I raced towards the Red Dam. Meeting mates for a game of war, the cricket stump I carried as a shotgun got stuck in my spokes, locking up my front wheel and flipping me face first into the road. Following my face into the asphalt was my left knee, then my right elbow, then my right knee and my left elbow. Then my face came back for seconds. The bike was bent; the cricket stump had snapped, and the footy card pegged to the spokes (which, when in motion, made my Malvern Star sound like a motorbike) was in shreds. I was not well. Somehow I managed to make it home. Horrified, Mum dabbed me with Dettol for days, using tweezers to pick the gravel from between my teeth.

CHAPTER THREE

The Pill

The rainbow football was my first. Made of white rubber, it had coloured stripes like a milky marble or a boiled lolly. Though too easily beaten by a rose bush or a dog's bite, it was nonetheless better than the brown plastic footies bought from giant baskets outside service stations. They hurt my toes and didn't spin properly. An old canvas Lyrebird ball that we'd found behind the local fruit shop lay abandoned in the yard. But it was at Chadstone Shopping Centre that I spotted a leather footy for sale and fell in love. Eleven dollars! With my weekly fifty cents in pocket money, this was way beyond my means.

Dad read books outside the café with the other men, all apparently waiting for their wives to stop spending. I mentioned the ball, and to my surprise, Dad asked me to show him the shop. And there, for no reason at all, he bought me the leather footy!! Nothing about it being an early birthday present or cutting down on what I got for Christmas. He just bought it for me. In the car heading home, I cradled it in my arms. It said 'Australian Rules

Football' in large letters on the side. With 'Made In India' underneath.

At Pinewood Primary, we played a new football game each day. Spread over three 'quarters', these games we umpired ourselves, paying only the most obvious free kicks. A punch in the face was generally penalised. Otherwise, it was open season. There were two games going on at any given time: one played by the attractive, talented kids down the length of the oval, the other played by me and my group of mates, across. The morning recess session started after we'd eaten our play lunch: Wizz Fizz, Snak Paks, pineapple doughnuts. The lunch-time leg followed a healthy dose of vegemite sandwiches.

Snak Paks were a special treat, especially the peaches. We quenched our thirst with Prima, or Hi-C if your Mum was a bulk-buyer. On warmer days I sucked on triangular, solid-ice Sunny Boys, but they made my lip bleed, and I never found a 'free', though I always looked inside for the winning yellow writing. Drinking the melted, ultra-sweet liquid at the bottom would send my sugar levels skyrocketing. It was like a dangerous drug in its intensity. Pity the poor teacher attempting to keep me under control in class after such an overload.

Our games were regularly interrupted at 'magpie' time of year by nesting birds, which would swoop on anyone walking past. Like customised bi-planes dropping water on a bushfire, the magpies attacked in a relentless barrage aimed at protecting their nests. Our pine-tree goal posts often doubled as a magpie's home, so after several high kicks had burst through the upper branches, we'd suddenly be sent scattering by a squadron of the hard-beaked bastards launching after us in furious formation like the helicopter scene from *Apocalypse Now*.

We picked new teams each morning from the same selection of kids. The pine-tree goals were near the fence. When the ball went over, whoever kicked it had to get it back — unless it was Fats. Fats was a classic. The wire mesh was only waist high, but he was unable to climb anything. Attempts at rolling himself over proved funny but fruitless. In order to save our time and his dignity, we took turns retrieving the ball on Fats' behalf. Fats had a swarthy complexion, and Armenian parents who encouraged a healthy appetite.

Fats was but one of our motley crew. Luciano was an enigma. Naturally muscular through loading his dad's vegetable truck on weekends at the Dandenong Market, he combined below-average ability with sporadic style. Luciano had a head of thick, dark curls which elderly women loved. He could play okay, but his coordination would often abandon him and he'd end up making outrageous errors, such as kicking the ball into his own head. On cohesive occasions, though, he displayed the most sensational skills we'd ever seen. It was rare, but worth waiting for. On rainy days, Luciano walked home with his hands held up in front of his face and moving together from left to right, as if they were windscreen wipers, making the 'whooshing' sound with his mouth as he went along.

Greg Battersea had bulging eyes and buck teeth and believed in three bites at the cherry. He suffered from rapid ear-wax build-up, requiring regular injections to keep the problem under control. Footscray's full forward at that stage, Shane Loveless, was on a brief run of brilliant form, and showmanship was his speciality. He never took a mark with one grab if four or five were possible. It was a technique that made standard marks look spectacular. Following suit on the school oval, Greg would tap the ball from one hand to the other for ages, but always denied it was deliberate. The trick was to convince your mates that the three bites were actually required, because a begrudging round of applause was always given for really good marks.

Two Aboriginal boys, Gavin and Dave, lived in the neighbourhood. Their mum and dad were white, and I'm not sure whether the boys had been taken from their parents or voluntarily put up for adoption, but they seemed as settled or unsettled as any other kid. Gavin and Dave were hilarious. Dave spoke slowly and softly, yet he could cut you down with a quip from fifty paces. Like a crocodile lurking still and silent for hours until an unsuspecting victim strolls by, Dave was prepared to wait for the right moment before making a killer, comic remark. Gavin, on the other hand, was loud and quick in word and deed. One day during a back-yard cricket match at our house, Gavin pulled off a masterful manoeuvre. Running in to bowl a quickie at my brother, Gavin bounced the ball too far over Simon's head and straight through a window. 'Smash!' Ever the quick thinker, Gavin didn't even break stride, but continued running, out the open gate, into the street and away. 'My tea's ready', he shouted as he disappeared from our sight, just as the ominous sound of approaching adult footsteps reached the back door.

When has a football heard its final siren? A well-worn favourite footy holds a million memories. Finally handballing mine into the bin was the emotional equivalent of putting the family dog down. Neither could speak for itself and both were eventually replaced. Our dog's health had deteriorated to the point where putting her to sleep was the only proper course. We loved Coco, and wished she could live longer, but she'd been around for sixteen years and it was time she bit the bullet. The eleven-dollar footy lasted almost four years. One day, I noticed a single split stitch. Within a week, it was an epidemic. The bladder haemorrhaged outside the skin into an ugly jaundiced bubble, throwing the whole thing out of shape. I was saddened to see it in such a state. The end had arrived.

Surviving a season without a footy was frustrating. I had a red, white and black football which I'd been steadily asking each member of the Saints side to sign, but it was intended as an ornament. Next birthday I gratefully accepted an unkicked Kookaburra. I'd hoped for a Sherrin, but this was still a step up the ladder. The brand-new ball, like the first one, presented me with a quandary. Only a poet could properly describe a new football's flawless perfection, its breathtaking beauty, its holy virgin hide. This early love of leather saw me treat a new ball with the care I took carrying hot cups of tea in to my Mum — all tongue out and tip-toes.

We had a kick on the street after school every day, the ball becoming scuffed and scratched from the road's rough surface. Normally this was not a problem, but it was unthinkable when it came to my precious present. I'd allow it to be kicked only on the lushness of the local oval. Walking there, though, friends called for a handball. What to do? I didn't want them bouncing it on the bitumen, because it deserved better, but I didn't want to say so in case I was called a nancy-boy. Within two weeks, we were out on the road again. The ball was scratched and scuffed and my predicament had passed.

The Kookaburra was okay, but I yearned for something better. Upon reaching age twelve, like my brothers before me I was presented with a magnificent metallic-blue Malvern Star bike. With it, I found a part-time job at the local chemist, delivering pills to old people. The money went towards a Ross Faulkner I fancied.

My footies were all lavishly looked after. In our laundry cupboard was a rag-bag full of torn T-shirts, old pairs of Dad's apple-catcher undies, and other sundry obsolete items of clothing. One of these dipped in Dubbin leather wax was perfect for polishing. It prevented the ball becoming waterlogged. Waiting for my footy to dry after a work-out in the wet was a worry. Keeping it pumped up was a priority. This delicate task involved using a special needle screwed into a bicycle pump. The needle, made of second-rate steel, needed Vaseline for easier entry; otherwise, it could snap in half when overheated. As I held the ball between my knees one day, giving it a few powerful pumps, the needle broke off inside the bladder. We heard it bouncing about in there from that day forward. A bunch of blind blokes could have beaten us 'cos it sounded like a cowbell.

Whether Ross Faulkner footies were better than Sherrins was an ongoing debate, our equivalent of Ford versus Holden. We knew Sherrin was favoured by the League, but as we could afford only the less expensive 'Rossy', it became a contender.

My football knowledge was unsurpassed. I have evidence to prove this. I knew every player's number on each club's list. I knew which club they'd come from, be it an interstate, local or opposition side. I knew player heights, weights and, in St Kilda's case, even girlfriends' names. Any question had an answer: how many grand finals has Geelong won and when?; name Hawthorn's Brownlow medallists?; who was 'Chicken' Smallhorn? So as a regular reader of *Inside Football*, I was exited to learn of a competition called 'Fifty Footy Questions'. I went to work immediately. One or two questions demanded some study, but all up, it was a cinch.

The following week, Mum met me at the school gates. We lived nearby, so this was unusual. Something was up. Morbid thoughts raced through my mind. 'Congratulations', Mum said, with a big smile. 'A man from *Inside Football* rang and said you've won yourself a

Sherrin.' As I walked with her, hearing all the details, my feet didn't touch the ground. First correct entry. Full marks out of fifty. I was the winner!

The Sherrin was sure-fire proof that I knew my stuff. And even better, it was a night-game ball. The golden colour reflected its worth. Dad drove me to the offices of *Inside Football*. We met the Editor, Tony Greenberg, whom I recognised from the mug shot that crowned his column. He shook my hand and passed me the prize. My head almost popped with pride. 'Well done, son', said Dad as we headed home. 'You're a fart smeller — I mean a smart feller.' The schoolyard argument was over. Sherrin reigned supreme.

CHAPTER FOUR

The Initiation

'I said Vic Bitter boy, not fuckin' Fosters', fumed the father, before whacking his son with a straight right to the jaw. Knocked unconscious for bringing back the wrong brand of beer. The boy must've been about fourteen. The cops came and carted the father off as his son was attended to by St John's Ambulance officers. Unrepentant, the drunken dad struggled as he was led away, shouting: 'If he'd only done like I asked!'. This was my introduction to the outer. It was round three, 1979.

That maiden visit to Moorabbin opened my eyes to an environment previously beyond my imagination. The language was vicious, vulgar, loud and lewd. The people were intense and intriguing. Even the ladies used rude words. Everyone gave their total attention to the action on the field. I spent more time studying the crowd's reaction than watching what inspired it. I found it hard to comprehend that this had been going on for years without me being aware of it.

Even the dunnies were different — pre-war brickwork, with the light not working and occasional shards of sun sneaking through the queue. There were no trough or individual urinals, with stray pubes to wash away, just a gutter on the ground with a hole at one end. We might have been pissing against a prison cell wall. The acidic odour was overwhelming. A stale ale sauna. Instead of standing around silently while they were having a slash or waiting for the space to do so, most men would offer opinions on the state of play. 'We gotta flatten that number five', opined the old man next to me, addressing no-one in particular. 'Yeah. I hope Sarau knocks the shit out of him', someone added from behind the cubicle door. 'Christ O'Mighty. A talking toilet!' said another in reply, to hearty laughter from the lads.

When I spotted the Moorabbin Library, we knew it was close. Simon manned the Melways, directing us towards our destination. Simon and I were best mates. By this time, he was old enough to be responsible for me on his own, yet barely a teenager himself, he was still young enough to be of a similar mind to me. St Kilda's home ground was in Linton Street, Moorabbin. Dad dropped us off outside, amid the stalls selling scarves, the *Football Record* boys and the people waiting in prearranged spots for friends to show up.

Across the road from the oval, high on the pure-white wall of a warehouse, someone had sprayed the word 'Fuck'. Full Stop. We saw it when we stepped out of the station-wagon. Not 'Fuck You' or 'Fuck The System'. They were at least logical. No, just 'Fuck'. There seemed to be a general lack of conviction, which given the graffiti's position, dead centre of a hundred feet wide, fifty feet high warehouse wall, was in stark contrast to the enormous effort the piece must have taken to achieve. I wondered how anyone could gain satisfaction from such a cryptic statement. In what context was it meant to be taken? We laughed at the word on the wall every home game from that day forward.

At the ground's gates, we paid the pensioner behind bars in his personal prison and the turnstiles clanked us through into a whole new world. Threading our way amongst the throng, I heard fleeting fragments of conversation, each new discussion being drowned out by the next as we wound our way around the ground: 'I know for a fact me carby's cactus, but he reckons me starter motor's stuffed as well …', 'They reckon Ernie Sigley decked Don Lane at the Logies but no-one's saying why …', 'So she said, "Yeah, well you could've phoned", and I thought, "I couldn't stand, let alone phone!", but of course I never said nothin' …', and so on.

I longed to hear a number of these separate conversational segments somehow form a seamless sentence. It was something I did with the telly if I was home alone. If I flicked from a news program to a wildlife documentary and then to a music show, for example, I might be lucky enough to hear: 'The Queen announced today that … a sexually aroused Bengal tiger … will perform before a sell-out crowd at Wembley this week'.

Simon and I weren't sure where to stand at first. We settled for the wing, as it gave a good view of the entire ground. I can't recall the other team or even the end result. It was the culture shock that was so seductive, and I savoured it more than the score. At the footy that day, for the first time in my life, I was consciously aware of 'happiness', the state of being happy. It wasn't that I'd been unhappy until this point. It was just that, until now, I thought sipping the froth from a freshly filled glass of Creamy Soda before the bubbles fizzled out was the best life had to offer. Here, though, was something else entirely.

As the weeks went on, we gravitated towards the most obvious centres of St Kilda support. With all its pomp and circumstance, the cheer squad, which had allocated seating, appeared to involve the strongest supporters in attendance. In fact, they were merely the most organised. The cheer squad called for contributors, but we were reluctant, because they needed help building the banner two nights a week. Despite our obsession, we lived too far away and, besides, we hated anything like hard work. We stepped back a bit and found some space.

A number of cliques assembled around the ground. The area behind the goals at Moorabbin was a community within itself. The Animal Enclosure was on the wing, between the two fenced-off tunnels that players and umpires went into and came out of. Then there was our area: standing room between the goal posts, fifteen feet from the fence at the grandstand end. The region consisted of around two dozen subdivisions, which merged into one when the game commenced. Unlike most sections of the crowd, ours was almost exclusively male. Like a rock band, our line-up varied from year to year. The definitive version was me, my brother Simon, Steve the postie (not *our* postie; that was Stan), Shane from Syndal Tech, and Young Jason.

Over the years, we got to know by sight other supporters in the area. There was a mutual respect among us for enduring such communal masochism. 'Doughnuts' (so named because he tossed them at the opposition players whenever he was angry) was an alcoholic with a sharp wit and the constant idiot grin of one who is apparently happy with his lot. One afternoon he arrived with an envelope full of hard-core pornographic snaps featuring him and his girlfriend. As he passed the photos around at half-time, embellishing them with unwanted dirty details, a pair of nearby policemen became suspicious. Realising he was about to be rumbled, he ran towards them. 'Look, I've been sent these in the post. She's married, see, and if I find out who's trying to blackmail me, I'm gonna finish 'em off, I promise ya. They must've been watching through a window or something.' It was stroke of genius. The cops fell for it. We struggled to remain straight-faced.

Loyalty to our team was one thing, but being beaten so badly on such a regular basis was not exactly entertaining. If it takes two to tango, St Kilda was lucky to manage a slow foxtrot. As a result, we tended to provide much of our own amusement. 'Chook' was perhaps the funniest of us all. With eyebrows meeting in the middle and a sleeveless Saints jumper worn over his flannel shirt, he unleashed such booming character assassinations of the opposition that they actually earned retaliation. 'I've seen better heads in a butcher's shop', Steve O'Dwyer, Melbourne's red-headed ruckman, was told. 'Come over here and say that', O'Dwyer replied, serving only to incite a further barrage of riotous abuse and Bronx cheers from the blokes behind the goals. After some time, things settled down somewhat, only for Chook, at the first semblance of order, to shout out: 'Ronald McDonald wants his hair back'. Amid the resultant surrounding teary-eyed hilarity, even Danny Frawley, St Kilda captain and O'Dwyer's opponent at the time, was seen to be laughing uncontrollably.

Chook's partner in crime, Scott, was an artistic type with a moleskin jacket. Such was his superior intellect, I suspected him capable of completing *The Age* crossword. Yet he was a genuine and endearing yobbo. Chook and Scott were like chalk and cheese, but they were as one in their abusive efforts. 'John West hates you, Salmon', they announced in unison to the overgrown Essendon forward, who stuck two fingers up at them in response.

If an unknown opposition player upset him, Chook would go with his ultimate insult: 'You tape up rats', implying a seriously perverted tendency towards both bondage and bestiality on the part of the target. Scott enjoyed referring to opposition players by the number on their back, implying that they weren't important enough to be known by name. The laughter induced by their increasingly inventive insults encouraged a competitive streak among surrounding supporters, each attempting to top the previous effort.

We were approached each week in the outer by a bloke to whom Simon gave the name 'Shunner'. His real name was a mystery, but his habits never changed. Out of nowhere he would appear, sneaking up beside us, speaking in a secretive fashion out of the corner of his mouth, avoiding eye contact and always surveying everything around him. A pillar of paranoia. He had a mouth like a fish, a slit that opened and closed, without lips. Under his navy-blue, diamond-stitched parka, he wore about fifteen badges, all featuring photos of previous Saints players. Unzipping his jacket and pulling it slightly open to one side, like a hustler selling stolen watches, he'd point out one of the blokes on the badges and say: 'They never should've got rid of Russell Greene', in reference to someone who had moved elsewhere many moons ago. Then, without another word, he'd walk away, shunning the possibility of any addition to the conversation, not to be seen until next Saturday. Simon often bumped into him at the Moonee Valley trots. Shunner would sneak up, suggest a winner and walk away. His fancies always finished first.

Another bloke we nicknamed 'Beeper', after the cartoon Telecom owl. Beeper suffered from every physical tic in the book, including — and this was the highlight — an audible 'blip'. The poor fella tried to stop himself, but to no avail. It's not unusual to encounter a stutter in society today, even the occasional facial twitch, low growl or non-stop blinking bonanza, but an uncontrollable audible 'blip' as a finale to all of the above is indeed rare. Unless you're playing Atari Tennis. It was spooky hearing such a sound emitted by a man. A machine, maybe. It was as if he'd swallowed a bellbird. 'Blip!'

The supporters in our area of the outer lacked sympathy. Upon sighting another side's star lying face down in the dirt, we showed no mercy. 'Dig a hole and bury him', 'Put him out of his misery' and the racecourse-related 'Bring out the screen!' were among the concerned suggestions. This general mentality, I suggest, was not confined to Moorabbin. Football as a metaphor features in many other male environments. Whenever a gorgeous girl walks by who is considered luscious but appears below the 'legal age', we can console ourselves and show signs of chivalry with a single sentence: 'Give her a couple more seasons'.

One of VFA side Sandringham's more eccentric supporters also followed the Saints. Known simply as 'Zebra' (Sandringham's emblem), he drank what must have been five cans a quarter. By quarter-time he would begin to sporadically utter the word 'zebra' in a gurgling, guttural, horror-movie monster voice, taking around thirty seconds from the 'Z' to the 'A' thus: 'ZZZZZZZZZEEEEEEEEEBBBBBBBBRRRRRRRRAAAAAAAA'. He never said anything else to anybody. It bothered me somehow that this man's mother must have had many hopes and dreams for her baby son, and yet here he was, forty years on, known for shouting the name of a striped horse.

CHAPTER FIVE

The Serious Stuff

A fight before the opening siren is always exciting. Having prepared the mind and body all week, the moment before the first bounce must be a time of high tension. As players jostle around the centre square, and zigzag across the ground to take up their positions, someone has only to slip in a sneaky one and it's on for young and old. Simon and I used to say, 'They must be serious', when this sort of fight occurred, as if the flying fists were an indication of St Kilda's absolute determination to win the game. We never asked ourselves why this wasn't always the case or even why players would need a fracas to fire them up. All we knew was it meant more for our money.

Undoubtedly, the Saints' most infuriating habit was the fast finish. This affliction affected not just individual games, but also entire seasons. After being behind all day, St Kilda often staged a last-quarter comeback. To anyone not at the match, the final scores then seemed to suggest a solid effort. 'I don't know what you're complaining about', other sides' supporters would say. 'To get within a couple of goals of the top team is a pretty good performance.'

Reducing the deficit from eight goals to three when the game is all but over and the opposition have moved down a gear seems to indicate players protecting their place in the side. Why did they have so much energy in reserve? Why was there a second wind if they'd already worked as hard as we expected them to? St Kilda scoring the final few goals became a regular occurrence.

Storming home at the end of the season was even more upsetting. Following a string of disastrous displays, St Kilda liked to win four of their last five games, thus 'playing a big part in shaping the final five (or six)', as the press patronisingly put it. Some sides wore black armbands in memory of a recently lost loved one. St Kilda should have worn them in memory of the previous season. 'We see this period as a launching pad for next year' or 'We're in a rebuilding phase', said a series of coaches keen on keeping their jobs. Alex Jesaulenko, Tony Jewell, Graeme Gellie, Darrell Baldock and Ken Sheldon all declared an end-of-season resurgence to be indicative of the club's destiny. Only Sheldon saw his remarks become reality.

The first game of a new season was always the most exciting for Saints' fans. Everything before that point was forgiven. The slate was clean. After this match, we might be on top of the ladder. It usually took until the fourth round for us to accept that the rot had not so much set in as remained. We realised that the players who had momentarily fooled us with different haircuts still played the same way, while others with new numbers were merely the battlers of old. Another season shot. Another dream denied. Despite constant poor performances, St Kilda had a solid support base throughout the 1980s, a loyalty that probably sent most of us slightly mad.

Consider the following scenarios:

- With the clock ticking into time-on in the final quarter, in a game that really matters, St Kilda loses the lead it has held all day. Supporters hurl their *Football Records*, beer cans and beanies onto the ground in disgust.
- The same situation, except this time, the game doesn't matter at all and a goal to the Saints sees the pendulum swing back in our favour seconds before the siren sounds. Supporters scramble to retrieve their *Football Records*, beer cans and beanies, having only moments ago hurled them onto the ground in disgust.
- St Kilda is leading by a long way with the game near its end. Supporters ironically shout, 'Percentage!', knowing full well that we are so far behind the pack, a win by the most massive of margins would still not move us up the ladder. However, at least the *Football Records*, beer cans and beanies are safe and sound.

The Obsession

Simon and I were obsessives in that we were unable to walk away. We wanted to do so on many occasions. We often swore we'd do something else the following Saturday, more as a protest at persistent poor performances than because any better options had arisen. Then, during the week, we'd discover that Bruce Duperouzel was returning from injury or that Gary Odgers had served his suspension, and there we'd be, standing behind the goals again, witnessing yet another walkover.

We rarely enjoyed ourselves, even when we won. This was because we cared so much that watching any match was murder, even if we were five goals in front with five minutes remaining. The prospect of losing yet another game was uppermost in our minds the entire time. Our grief at being beaten saw us spiral into deep depression, despite being beaten on a regular basis. Mum's approach to us upon returning home for dinner differed according to the outcome. A win would see her waiting outside in the declining light, waving a St Kilda scarf shouting 'What a bottler!'. Then she'd serve us grilled cutlets and we'd chat about the game.

Mum and Dad were always delighted for us when we'd won. They seemed thrilled themselves. After all, with two fanatics in the house, they had little choice but to follow the Saints' fortunes. And a victory could be relished only after the final siren had sounded. These evenings, however, were few and far between. A more common Saturday night scenario would see us silently sloping inside, shattered by the sight of our team being hopelessly outplayed for the hundredth time.

Our family had a money-saving system whenever we wanted a lift home from the train station. We'd phone our house, let the phone ring three times, then hang up.

Unless somebody answered, the call didn't cost a cent. Dad would wait for our code after each game. Should somebody else ring at the same stage, he'd wait four or five rings before answering, to make sure. Some days, when St Kilda had been really, really badly whipped, Dad bypassed the whole procedure and was already there in the car as our train pulled in.

There were times when we knew our side would not succeed even before we surfaced on a Saturday morning. In ten years of traipsing out to Windy Hill, for example, we'd never come close to winning. Essendon always had the game tied up by quarter-time. It rained all day, so we'd be drenched even if under shelter. The ground wasn't so named for nothing. Yet we went along anyway and we stayed until the end, every time. On these occasions, we could feel the cold cutting through us. Back at the house, we'd huddle in front of the heater while soup was made. Nothing is as warm as a win on a wet winter afternoon, but St Kilda supporters had to rug up regularly.

Why did we, along with a few thousand other supporters, willingly suffer such anguish? Why did we never take one look out the window, one look at the selected sides and sensibly decide to stay in? Admittedly, there was a sense of pride involved. Following fearful thrashings in frightful conditions, friends never neglected to ask if we'd been to the game, even though they already knew the answer. While I was aware they thought us insane, I imagined they also found our undying loyalty endearing. I took satisfaction in knowing a surprise win by the Saints would make Simon and I the talking point of friends and family.

Sometimes, people I knew who supported other sides would make excuses for their inability or unwillingness to watch their team in action more often. Whenever somebody was going on about how great their team was on the weekend, I liked to ask if they'd actually seen the game, then watch as they attempted to avoid the question. With Melbourne being so football mad, some people foolishly felt guilty about not actively supporting their favoured side, as if not attending football matches was a sure sign of social ineptitude. Pretentiously, I used every opportunity to exploit these insecurities. Why should they have felt bad about having something better to do with their lives? Why would a sane person waste a wet winter weekend watching sport when they could snuggle up with a bottle of scotch? I didn't know the answer to such questions, but I enjoyed inducing such feelings of inferiority, if only because it levelled out my own lunacy.

Looking back on those black days, I still find it difficult to understand exactly why the Saints were so often second-rate. Regulars in the side included Trevor Barker, Jeff Cunningham, Greg Burns and Robert Elphinstone, all of whom had been selected at some stage to represent Victoria in the State of Origin games. The bearded Jeff Dunne twice won the Best and Fairest and cemented himself as one of the Big V's resident back pockets,

Geelong's Ian Nankervis playing almost permanently as the other. You may remember Jeff Dunne. His jet-black hair matched a beard, moustache and sideburns ensemble that appeared to be one whole piece. In fact, members of the band Devo were wearing something similar, so we wondered if Jeff Dunne was a fan. Roy Ramsay, a North Melbourne defender, had exactly the same jet-black hair ensemble, probably purchased from the same shop. Towards the end of Jeff Dunne's St Kilda career, he took to growing his hair longer, which made him look a bit like Peter 'G'day!' Russell 'G'day!' Clarke. 'Where's the cheese?', we'd shout whenever he went near the ball.

At times, I'm almost embarrassed by what remains in my memory. If I removed some of the irrelevant rubbish from my mind, there might be more room for matters of substance. I probably have a greater recollection of Jeff Dunne's Handball Championship achievements than does Jeff himself. As starving men become appreciative of mere morsels, desperate football supporters make the most of small mercies. If a Sun Superkick winner, purely by virtue of living in the right suburban zone, represented St Kilda, we celebrated the success. The first thing I thought of when we signed up Geoff Ablett from Hawthorn was that he was the half-time sprint supremo. Never mind that he was a wonderful wingman from a very successful side, who would instantly strengthen our centre line. What mattered more was that when it came to the long break in the last game of the league season, we were a certainty.

If the problem was a lack of key position players, then it should have been solved by the emergence of Tony Lockett at full forward and Danny Frawley at full back, so it can't have been that. Whatever the reasons, all I knew was for sure was that whenever St Kilda won, it was treated by everybody as an upset, no matter who we beat.

CHAPTER SIX

The First Time

'Call me Trevor.' That's what he said, word for word. Not Eddie or Adam or Ishmael, but Trevor, as in Trevor Barker.

I was sitting alongside him in the empty grandstand at Moorabbin during an unannounced pre-season intra-club practice match. For footballers, the intra-club practice match is the equivalent of a fire drill. For spectators, it's the most boring event they will ever witness. Still, a few supporters were scattered around the ground, knowing they'd at least see a St Kilda victory. I had no idea about etiquette, and Barker didn't seem to mind, so I continued firing off questions, using his surname as we did at school.

'Barker? Do you reckon we'll make the finals this year?', I pestered. 'Barker? Are you gonna go for the Brownlow?', and so on. 'Call me Trevor', he said. First-name basis. Brilliant! 'Trevor? Is it true you almost signed with Collingwood last season?'. On and on I went. He kept answering, which only encouraged me. It must have been a nightmare. Not just me and not just here, but everybody, everywhere.

Trevor Barker became even more of an obsession for me than the St Kilda Football Club itself. My idolisation emerged because I wanted to *be* him. Professionally and personally, Barker inspired fantasy. He made us feel good. A man who makes men want to follow in his footsteps and women want to fool around with him. The directing of my total attention towards Trevor was not at all embarrassing at the time, though in hindsight I do feel foolish. When he broke a bone, I sent a get-well card to the club. Upon selection for the State side, I'd convey my congratulations. Any excuse for communication was exploited.

Dear Trevor,
Hope your exploratory knee surgery went well.
Look forward to seeing you play for the Saints
again soon.

Best wishes from
Matthew Hardy

My correspondence always received a hand-written reply, which only made things worse. Like Kathy Bates' character in the movie *Misery*, who claimed to be her hero's 'number one fan'. My pursuit was almost pathological.

Mum secretly arranged for Barker to phone me on my thirteenth birthday, to wish me all the best. I can't imagine how she arranged it, but he agreed to the idea. I was in my room when Mum called me to the phone. When he announced his name, I refused to believe it was true. I suspected one of my big brother's mates, and began the guessing game, running through all the names I knew. Finally, the voice assured me it was truly Trevor Barker, and as I realised what was happening, I couldn't breathe. This was easily the most exciting moment of my life. What did he say? I have no idea. I cared only that it was Barker who said it.

CHAPTER SEVEN

The Fantasy

'And Hardy marks! Could he be the hero? Fifty feet from goal, on an acute angle. St Kilda five points behind with only seconds remaining in what has been a glorious, hard fought grand final. They've come from five goals down in only fifteen minutes. Can Collingwood lose from such a commanding position? The siren sounds!! Hardy must kick accurately if the Saints are to collect the premiership cup. He's scored ninety-nine so far this season. Will this be a fairytale finish? The spectators are spilling over the fence. There's nothing the police can do at this point. Hardy lines up his shot. He kicks, an it's straight through the big sticks!!! St Kilda snatches victory. Hardy had kicked his hundred. Chaotic scenes here at the MCG as the crowd invades the arena. I've not seen anything like it in all my time. They're chanting Hardy's name as he is chaired around the ground'.

Give me and my football a moment alone and this was the scenario my imagination invented. It wasn't difficult. I knew the script sideways. Sometimes I went the whole way and made the successful shot a banana kick. The banana kick is the Aussie Rules equivalent of cricket's reverse sweep. Unreliable, risky and attempted only by renegades or champions. The ball is held horizontally in the hand and kicked on the inner end, curving in a semi-circle away from the body. To win a game with it would be the ultimate evidence of steel balls. To miss in the same situation? Sporting suicide.

Call me irresponsible. I practised the banana kick until my feet bled. A poor percentage pierced the goal posts, and I never improved my performance from the almost impossible position of behind the boundary line, deep in a forward pocket. Achieving precision under such circumstances was pointless, as the opportunity to take a similar shot in a real game almost never arose. Still, where was the fun in scoring six points by yourself from right in front?

In fact, I practised every key footy skill with equal gusto. I hung a tyre on our back gate and tried to handball through the hole. I took our Totem Tennis pole apart and swapped the tennis ball for my footy, swinging it around and taking marks from every angle. I tied one end of a long elastic string to a house brick and the other to my Sherrin's laces, short-passing to its full stretch, then gathering the ball on the run when it rebounded. To increase my coordination, I borrowed from a Darrell Baldock idea I'd read, running repeatedly around the house while bouncing two footies. I improved my leap by adjusting the Hills Hoist higher each time I managed to touch the wire. Even now as I write, I wonder why I wasn't rewarded. It was all to no avail. What frustrated me most was the fact that the skills I so desperately sought were often served up to people who had no wish for them.

A kid called Alex Ferrari once played for our primary school football side when a couple of other kids were away on camp. One of the first kids to have his hair cut in tails, Alex hated the game, but we were desperate to make up the numbers and he was somehow coaxed away from the soccer team. We quickly discovered he was a magnificent mark and a great kick. He marked everything that came his way, kicked six goals and would have played even better if he'd known the rules. We had to explain why the man was standing on the mark, how to line up for a shot, which sticks to kick the ball between. The bastard was better than the rest of us — and we'd been playing all our lives! It seemed so unfair.

The Learning

Weekend footy clinics on our primary school oval were where it all began. Every Saturday morning in mid-winter, a small group of devoted dads arrived at the crack of dawn to run us through a series of basic drills designed to slowly and surely improve our coordination. These, of course, were the same dads who always showed up whenever a working bee was arranged. As we arrived in the early morning mist, many of the mums on the sidelines remarked on the likeness between Wayne Bulte and myself.

Wayne and I were classmates, with St Kilda in common. Much to my dismay, Wayne and Trevor Barker shared the same birthday, 7 October. Trust my parents not to have consulted the calendar before I was conceived. Sporting identical haircuts and the same skinny frame, Wayne and I both wore Saints shorts, socks, and jumpers with the number '1' sewn on the back, as worn by our preferred player. There the similarities ended, however, for as soon we started the training session, Wayne's superb skills separated us straight away.

Fitzroy ruckman Ron Alexander appeared at our final footy clinic, to hand out Participation Awards. We assumed the word 'participation' referred to a certain degree of skill, but as one kid after another was asked to come up and accept a certificate, it gradually dawned on us that these accolades were simply for regular attendance. Though our names were each typed onto a piece of quality cartridge paper, it was all something of a disappointment, involving neither happiness nor humiliation for anyone. At the close of proceedings, with forty to fifty kids having been given their 'awards', one burst into tears.

While not exactly a star, Justin Kettle was as average in ability as any of the boys. However, due to an unfortunate clerical error, his name had escaped the list, so he was left empty-handed. He immediately believed he hadn't made the grade, as did all the other kids. If even one person wasn't good enough to pass the test, then obviously, the rest of us were. A teacher hurried the devastated youngster away into an office to correct the terrible mistake, but the damage had already been done. The Participation Award suddenly took on a whole new significance. Despite the adult's explanations, we remained convinced that we were better than somebody else. Justin's confidence never recovered.

Ron Alexander lived near our school and was persistently pestered by neighbourhood footy fanatics. With a few friends in tow, I dutifully knocked on his door one afternoon during the off-season to ask for an autograph. Undeterred by the sound of Mrs Alexander saying, 'Ron! It's another bunch of bloody kids again', we waited until he answered the door and beckoned us through into the back garden, where he was enjoying a couple of cold cans with Fitzroy full back Chris Hansen. Even to our young eyes, they seemed well-oiled. Both signed our books, Alexander saying: 'There's a bonus for you boys. Two for the price of one'. Then he burped and sent us on our way. It was an eye opener. It was beyond our comprehension that footy players might also be someone's father, brother, husband, son. That they were as liable to maintain a marriage as the next man or had to remember to make the car repayments on time had never entered our heads. Surely, these men were superhuman. None of us mentioned what was on our minds. It was better, we felt, to forget the facts with which we'd been confronted.

It wasn't the first time I'd actively avoided the truth. Mum once took me to Brandon Park Shopping Centre to see Humphrey B. Bear. I must've been four years old. As he lifted me up for a cuddle, I polished his nose with my hankie. As Humphrey bent to put me down, I saw a man inside his black mesh eye-holes. Either I refused to accept what I'd seen or it was too confusing for my little mind to manage, but given the choice, I went with fiction and ignored the fact. Humphrey remained real.

Mark Lee also visited our school, as a League promotions man. As we were in Richmond's recruiting zone, a Richmond supporter had sent a letter requesting that the Tiger ruckman make an appearance. His head almost touched the ceiling as Mrs Attica, our elderly vice-principal, escorted him around the corridors. I'd never seen anyone so tall before. Outside on the oval, despite his attempt to take us through a number of designated training drills, all we wanted to see was how far he could kick.

Known as 'The General', Lee had endeared himself to supporters of all sides with his efforts in a series of Australia versus Ireland Gaelic football games. The games were played according to a compromised set of rules that welded the Irish way of playing with our own. The end result was like two teams playing rugby with a soccer ball. Still, it provided an opportunity to showcase Aussie Rules internationally. Alongside Gary McIntosh — a belligerent full back from South Australia, with wild eyes and a goatee beard — Mark Lee caused wholesale, random destruction in Dublin with his use of the 'coat-hanger'. The General's method of using a forearm to the throat to stop an oncoming player in possession was somehow within the new laws, and while it won us the series, I wonder in hindsight about the wisdom behind a British colony upsetting the Irish.

The success of local footy clinics led to VFL-organised Superclinics, with selected footy stars showing us kids how it was done. They handed out booklets called *How To Realise Your Dream To Become A Football Star*. The booklets didn't work. I know. I read mine religiously.

Aside from the stars themselves, the specially planned afternoons were often understaffed, so several lucky kids became assistants. I was Trevor Barker's right-hand man at one such event and became head of the witches hats! I placed them precisely as I was told, and at the end, he ruffled my hair as a reward. It was due recognition, because on past occasions, I'd always ended up in groups supervised by some unknown Under 19s player. How much weight would their opinion carry with a VFL coach when passing on reports of my superb yet undiscovered skills? Naïvely, I thought the Superclinics were thinly veiled recruiting sessions, rather than the PR exercises they really were.

Formed to encourage kids along to the footy, the VFL Junior Supporters' Club was a fine idea. Kellogg's Corn Flakes boxes carried a coupon on the back. Once filled in and sent to the correct address, a membership card duly arrived, entitling the owner to free entry at any five games that season. There was no limit on the number of members per household, which led to people sending in four or five coupons under different names, ensuring they paid no admission for the entire season. The age limit (fifteen) was rarely policed at the grounds, so it wasn't unusual to see beer guts and facial hair among the queue of kids at the Junior Supporters' Club entrance gates.

First thing on Sunday mornings, Channel Seven screened the Junior Supporters' Club TV show, on which I'd watch out for my club member's card number, in case I won a prize. I'd been in it for two whole seasons without winning a thing. Then my next-door neighbour, whom I'd coaxed into joining in the first place, won a Saints lunch box on his second Sunday. I didn't speak to him for a week.

The Torment

Mondays at school were a nightmare if my team had lost on the weekend. Kids sought me out so they could sing the score and other such stuff. As soon as the siren sounded on a St Kilda victory, I'd start thinking about the kids at school who barracked for the team we'd just beaten. They'd given their share. I'd endured it from all angles. Some kids kept on for ages, but as soon as I started asking them to shut up, the whole class would gather together and grab each other's thumbs, one on top of the other in a type of totem pole. Then, moving all the hands at once in a circular motion, as if holding a giant spoon, they'd chant: 'Hardy's in a stir, stir, stir. Hardy's in a stir, stir, stir', until I either calmed down or shouted out: 'I am not!!'.

Variations on well-known songs were sung sometimes by the girls if they wanted to annoy the boys. 'Waltzing Matilda, boo for St Kilda, down with the magpies and up with the blues.' Various adjustments were made to the lyrics, according to the respective allegiances of the singer and their target.

For me, school's major role was as the easiest way to meet up with my mates. Try getting five, six or even more friends into the one room once you're an adult and see how long it takes. Under the age of fifteen, there's no work worries, no cash crisis, no partner to consult and few, if any, transport requirements. Each new year saw another curious combination of characters with whom you'd spend the next twelve months. Aside from the occasional animosities, I either got on well with my classmates or else we left each other alone.

The Testing Time

Grade Five saw the ultimate high arrive. We actually drove a teacher mental. We tended to test a new teacher out almost immediately. Before earning a classroom's respect, new teachers had to pass an exam more exhausting than anything they'd ever put to their students. Any chink in their emotional armour was exploited.

Miss Helfen survived just three days of torment before throwing in the towel. She looked like the stereotypical librarian. She did well to survive the afternoon when all of us reflected the sun off our watches straight into her face, yet her persistence merely encouraged us to pick up the pace. We were actually singing a derisory song at the moment she shoved everything off her desk onto the floor and disappeared, never to be seen again.

A trouble-shooter promptly showed up in her place. Mrs Sherman had obviously been brought in to do a job, and announced upon arrival that she was not to be messed with. Far from making us tremble, this was treated as a challenge. It was Janine Towers' porno pictures that saw off Mrs Sherman, whom we called Fearless Fly, after the cartoon character, because her eyes seemed to shrink whenever she removed her coke-bottle glasses. This time, it took us two weeks.

We knew she was close to the edge when she dragged a girl out of her chair by the hair and into the headmistress' office just for answering back. While the two of them were out of the room, Janine Towers held up a copy of *Playboy* she'd found in the playground. Janine suffered from a million permanent mozzie bites and was very boy-like in her behaviour. Bruce Weiser, who liked to imitate car engines, varying his tone according to what 'gear' he was in at the time, told Janine that if she didn't flick through all the pages for everyone to see, he'd tell the teacher what was going on. As Janine complied, Bruce reacted in his car-engine vocabulary, revving his motor harder as each new naked woman unfolded before him.

Already seething, Mrs Sherman returned to a sound and sight extravaganza which was by that point beyond explanation. Clapping, laughing, cheering, jeering, a human gear-box going berserk. 'That's it! I have had it!', she screamed, tucking her things under her arm. 'They were right!' The door slammed. We had exceeded even our own expectations. I suppose we were proud of the achievement. I don't recall any degree of guilt. After all, driving a teacher mad was every kid's ambition. Students from classes known to have done so were held in high regard by their peers.

When Mrs Woods walked in, we were on a hat-trick. She had short, straight, dark hair and endearing saucepan-sized eyes, as if she'd been animated by a Japanese artist. Vice-principal Mrs Attica, looking like an ageing, unkempt Margaret Thatcher, introduced us to our new victim with a damning speech, which began by labelling us a 'herd of elephants' and ended with a dire warning of the discipline devised just for us if we failed to show good manners. Then she disappeared out the door, her footsteps followed by the sound of twenty-five trunks trumpeting in our best impression of an elephant herd.

'Righto', said Mrs Woods, as if nothing out of the ordinary had just happened. 'I'll get to know you all as I go along, but for now, my first task is to organise a footy-tipping competition. As I go around the room, I want you to tell me your names and the team you barrack for.'

Her immediate appeal to a common denominator — football — coupled with her round, friendly face, floored us all. There was no raising of eyebrows at each other or shrugging of shoulders as if to say, 'It's an interesting approach. Let's give her a chance'. We actually forgot about giving her shit. That year ranks among the best of my school life. She was the first teacher I'd known to ask that we each bring a plate of something on the last day of school. Most of us brought fairy bread and a packet of chips, but the rich kids arrived with Chocolate Royals, the Crown Lager of biscuits. I liked eating crinkle-cut chips one crinkle at a time, from left to right, enjoying this procedure only marginally more than wearing Cheezels on my fingers like rings.

Chancing upon gigantic Twisties or chips in a packet, Mark, Simon and I kept them as trophies on top of the telly. If you'd seen any of them, you'd have known they were too special to eat. When sharing our Samboys, we always placed the green ones and the burnt bits on top before offering the packet to Mum and Dad, hoping they wouldn't look at their selection en route to their mouths. When bored, we'd put the empty packets in the oven and watch them shrink, before poking a hole in the corner and using them as key rings.

Mrs Woods even gave Simon and me a lift to the game when St Kilda played Footscray at the Western Oval that season. We asked to be dropped off about a mile from the ground, in case anyone from school saw us getting out of the car. She'd earned our respect, but there was no need to suck up.

Kick-to-Kick

The end of a school day meant organising my own movements until teatime. Then Mum and Dad took over responsibility until it was the teacher's turn again the next day. Having a kick on the street was the easiest option. By myself or with a mate was fine, but ideally, there were two kids up each end. One of the pair indicated where they wanted the ball. We'd either take off on a quick lead or point skyward, meaning we wanted to contest the mark. I'd volunteer my back as a stepladder if someone up the other end 'put it up' for a friend to fly for. Then we'd swap positions so I could have a go at glory.

I tried to emulate Con Gorozidis, a flamboyant forward-pocket player for the Saints, who specialised in putting both hands on his opponent's shoulders to boost himself for a spekky. The rules allowed such stunts, as long as you held the mark. More often than not, Gorozidis ended up *on* the mark, after his effort failed and he'd given away a free kick. Gorozidis also had a strange way of shooting for goal. He preferred to be running across the face and away from the sticks so he could kick as if snapping one over the shoulder. Even when lining up for a set shot from right in front, he always managed to take his kick in a similar style. Whether he wanted to make his every move seem sensational or whether it was a technical flaw, I'm not sure. Maybe he was influenced by someone he'd seen as a youngster. Either way, I adopted his methods myself.

A family of St Kilda supporters lived over the road from us, the Tilleys. Damon and Nathan, the younger two of three boys, were good blokes and about the same age as Simon and me. Damon had distinctive white spots on his brown hair where the pigmentation wasn't there, while

Nathan was a sandy blonde who looked like someone from an earlier era, as if he should always be viewed in sepia tones. I don't know if it was the way he squared his shoulders or what, but whenever I saw group photos of Olympians from the 1940s and 1950s, I half expected to spot Nathan.

We got along well, yet despite our red, white and black alliance, we never really became great mates. It may have been because we were only ever allowed lemon cordial in their house. The Tilleys had white carpet fitted throughout the house. Therefore it was not in Mrs Tilley's interests to have kids spilling brightly coloured drinks all over the place. It made sense, but it didn't make friends. Call me spoilt, but if I couldn't have a raspberry or lime cordial, then I'd have to hang out somewhere else. Besides, Mrs Tilley was a member of the Pinewood Tennis Club, the committee of which was always able to find a new rule preventing Mark, Simon and me from joining. Simon had to use his Bjorn Borg Donnay racquet and Slazenger ball against a nearby service-station wall.

From time to time during a kick-to-kick, an old bloke looking for a laugh on his way to the shops for some smokes would break his walking rhythm, veer off the footpath and trot out onto the road towards us, offering a tentative lead. We always obliged, though barely resisted the urge each time to boot the footy at them full bore.

Poorly placed power lines were always on our footy's flight path. Whenever the ball hit the wrong cable,

Mr Waylaars came out in his unbuttoned pyjamas to complain about us ruining his TV reception. Why didn't the council consult the kids about putting in the telegraph poles, we wondered? Where were our rights? Mr Waylaars drank a bottle of beer on his back porch each morning for breakfast. He owned a sausage dog called Fritz, which knew how to wait at the traffic lights until the coast was clear before crossing. Fritz didn't actually press the button, but we were still impressed. Mr Waylaars enjoyed playing the organ after an occasional ale, and had a collection of albums by famous German organists, though I suspect not even he could tell one of those albums from another.

Cars presented us with another problem. Stationary or otherwise, they got in the way, and were to be avoided, in case the ball did the vehicle damage. I despised drivers who parked outside our house. It restricted our enjoyment and left limited room to send a torpedo sailing. Moving cars were also a cause for concern. Watching each other's backs, we used a clever code to warn of oncoming traffic, calling out: 'Car!' whenever we saw one approaching. This method was very effective.

Respect for players on teams other than yours was reflected in the linking of a player's name with a particular skill, whether it be taking a spekky, mastering the torpedo or scoring a magical goal. Shouting the right surname at the right moment was what was required here. Thus, a high mark might prompt a cry of 'Knights!', 'Bosustow!' or, best of all and coming a close second to

'Cattogio' in the enunciation stakes, 'Van der Haar!'. Any player launching into a 'torp' required calls of 'Quinlan!', 'Blight!' or, and in this case always using his whole name, 'Jimmy Jess!'. Most of us enjoyed doing a 'Manassa' when we had the chance, though the only thing anybody knew about him was 'that run' down the ground. We gravitated towards the glamour of forwards and followers. No-one ever yelled 'Malarkey!' when spoiling a mark.

The Post Match Punt

While a kick on the road outside the house is good fun, the ultimate is a kick on the ground after a real game. Running around the same turf your heroes had trodden only ten minutes earlier was marvellous. Recreating the action gave us goosebumps. At Moorabbin we'd kick in front of the social club. I confess to trying my best in the hope that some talent scout might spot my skills through the windows and sign me up! I thought this way right up to the age of seventeen, not realising until the time I entered the social club myself that the people inside were all too pissed by that point to see themselves in the mirror, let alone sight a potential back-pocket champion outside.

Luciano and I had once made a similar mistake when having a kick at a local oval. An old man wearing a cardigan appeared out of nowhere, walking a Dalmatian. Smoking a pipe, he stood watching for a while, which convinced us he was a talent scout of some kind. Sure enough, after witnessing our scintillating skills, he called for us to come over.

'You two look like fit young fellas. You like exercise do you?' We nodded in reply. 'Listen, why don't the two of you sprint to those goal posts and back again and I'll time you? Okay? On the count of three.' Away we went, busting a gut to be the first back. It was a dead heat, and he said, 'Forty-two seconds. Not bad'. Then, instead of asking either of us to sign a contract as we'd hoped, he requested that we both take off our T-shirts and show him our shoulders. 'Get stuffed!' we responded in unison, before bolting, though in truth we were more upset at having not been recruited by a top footy club than at his strange suggestion.

After any VFL game, we'd swarm onto the ground the second the siren sounded. Following a mad sprint to reach the centre circle first, a flock of footballs flew. The danger was, another ball might fly at full pace into your face while you kept an eye on your own. Simon copped more than his fair share. Footies towards his forehead were like moths to a flame.

CHAPTER EIGHT

The Media

Mr Wise lived over the road. He and his wife were Indian, both teachers, and the most peaceful people I'd ever met. Mr Wise (who looked like Indian cricketer Dilip Doshi, then one of the world's finest spin bowlers) always offered us cashews to eat, which made us think he was wealthy. They had a colour TV before anyone else in our street, and let us watch it.

My original fancy for footy coincided with the introduction of colour television. With its ripe red ball and luscious green grass, Aussie Rules football exploded onto our screens like never before, creating a growing demand for mass coverage. Ratings rose across the board. The 1970s saw the first 'live' VFL grand final telecast and the first televised Brownlow Medal count. This merchandising molehill was to become a mountain.

In the view of me and my mates, Peter Landy was the worst of all the commentators on television. His opinions carried no weight with us, because he hadn't played senior footy himself. (Note, however, that this same fact didn't stop us from assuming *we* knew everything about the game.) Even though we didn't like Landy, we were obviously influenced by his style. It was he who inspired the excitedly shouted surname. His unbridled enthusiasm as someone soared skyward was infectious. 'Barker.' At such moments, he forgot he was a commentator and became a member of the crowd. In hindsight, for all our criticism, Peter Landy made a fine contribution. Without him, football coverage in the 1970s would not have been the same. Some of the most memorable marks from that era look less magical on the replays simply because he isn't calling them. Viewing the classic marks he didn't call on video is like seeing the shark scenes from 'Jaws' without the double-bass in the background — devoid of emotional content.

Lou Richards was more elaborate. A former Collingwood premiership captain, he created a huge number of now-famous nicknames and made himself familiar with the top footy stars. Through his articles in *The Sun* and his role as an all-round football personality for Channel Seven, Richards promoted the game relentlessly. North Melbourne's rotund ruckman Mick Nolan became known as 'The Galloping Gasometer', after the gigantic gasworks which overshadowed the Kangaroo's Arden Street ground. Geelong's 'Jumping' Jack Hawkins was so called because of his legendary leap. Carlton's champion defender Bruce Doull was dubbed 'The Flying Doormat', due to his wild, scruffy appearance and acrobatic defensive deeds. Aboriginal umpire Glenn 'Jesse' James' nickname was born from the 'quick draw' of his pencil from his pocket when recording a reportable incident.

Footy seasons could tend to stagnate during the middle stages, which was when Louie spiced things up with one of his public dares. His motivation may have been the improvement of his own already significant public profile and personal status, but it also forced the spotlight onto the game itself. One bad bet led to Lou rowing then Geelong coach Billy Goggin down the Yarra in a bathtub, another to his cleaning of Footscray's main street with a toothbrush, supervised by Teddy Whitten.

The public's increasing appetite for footy news led to the media progressively fixing the microscope on players' private lives, not so much the sleazy side as their occupations, their non-sporting interests, and their opinions on everything from washing powder to world peace. Much was made of the few footballers with evidence of an outstanding education. Carlton captain Mike Fitzpatrick, we were often informed, was a Rhodes Scholar who had studied at Oxford, and so was held in high esteem as a tactician. Carlton's aristocracy approved of his appointment in much the same fashion as England enjoyed the upper-class credentials of its then cricket captain, Mike Brearley. Dual Brownlow medallist Peter Moore (who looked, from side on, like Punch *and* Judy) graduated as a mature-age honours student from Monash University, with photographs of him in his mortar board duly printed in Melbourne newspapers.

The game's scandalous side was left more or less alone, except for one weekly newspaper, *The Truth*. An indication of its editorial policy is given by its headline: 'Sir Billy Dies on the Job', a reference to the unfortunate circumstances in which Bill Sneddon, politician and Melbourne footy club president, left this life. *The Truth* ran a regular column under the by-line of Richmond's legendary 'Captain Blood', Jack Dyer. Its title was 'Dyer 'Ere'. (Diarrhoea! Get it?) Obviously, they were aiming a couple of levels lower than was *The Age*, but at fifteen, I found the joke worth a very loud laugh every week. At that age, *The Truth* was difficult to get a gander at, as they always ran the most scandalous story on the front page, often featuring then footy superstars Des Tuddenham or Len Thompson, with the continuation on page two. Reading page two meant exposing the bare boobs on page three, and as the lady in our local newsagency knew Mum, I needed to be sly and swift whenever I wanted to scan the paper without buying it.

No-one I actually knew had ever been in the papers or on the telly until our Grade Three teacher, Mr Ilton (whose circulation-threatening wedding ring indicated how hefty he'd grown in the years since becoming a husband), hit the small screen by making it through as a contestant on *Sale Of The Century*. Host Tony Barber, a Carlton man, made his traditional bouncing and kicking entry to the set and then, in the introductions, made mention of Pinewood Primary. Mr Ilton promptly said 'Hello' to the students. We were officially on the map!

Soon after, an Arab kid moved in around the corner from us. Walla (I didn't know whether that was his first or last name) was a year older than I and went to my school, but we hadn't met in the month since his arrival in the neighbourhood. One day, we saw his dad invited to 'Come on down!' by Ian Turpie on *The New Price Is Right.* Mr Walla won a moped and, shortly afterwards, his son began riding it around the nearby side-streets on quiet Sunday afternoons. Extremely envious, I went round to his house and, after a pleasant ten minutes, asked him if I could have a go on his moped. He said no, so I punched him. I hadn't planned to do it. It just happened, and I went home. The surrounding suburbs and everyone within them seemed to be surging forward while I was being left behind.

Even Mr Donnelly next door had been on *The Don Lane Show*, interviewed in relation to his expertise in the computer industry. We sat through all that 'Nice to see you. To see you nice' shit until our neighbour's turn in the spotlight arrived. He was good, but Uri Geller had been on earlier, bending spoons, which was always going to be a hard act to follow. Then the Lanky Yank finished up with his 'I love your faces' sign language stuff and it was all over. The man next door was *on the telly*. I saw him in a different light from that day forward.

The World of Sport

Sundays would not have been the same without Uncle Doug, spruiker extraordinaire, advertising Patra orange juice, Ballantyne chocolates, Delmonte suits and Tosca bags on the weekly edition of Channel Seven's *World of Sport*. WOS had the commonsense to have Aussie Rules football as its main focus. Televised only in Victoria, it wouldn't have lasted twenty-six years otherwise. Aside from the advantage of being able to feature footage from the previous day's play (this being in an era when all games were played on a Saturday), WOS served as a blueprint to today's *Footy Show* and its imitators, but was vastly superior, mainly because the obvious effects of alcohol intake were on display. Cold cans and meat pies were laid on for presenters and guests, so that the studio each Sunday resembled an office Christmas party. Presenters were known to pause mid-sentence so they could ask those off-screen to keep the noise down. Televised live, a series of innovative and intriguing segments formed the framework for WOS's somewhat shambolic sporting commentary.

There were some non-football segments, such as the racing segment, fronted by Bill Collins, 'the Accurate One', with interviews of helium-voiced jockeys thanking 'Mr Hayes for everyfink', and the wood-chopping segment, where large men in checked shirts or singlets balanced on logs to fight it out in the studio, their axe-wielding skills backed by the voice of legendary lumberjack Jack O'Toole.

Then there was the soccer. The mid–1970s and early 1980s were halcyon days for the fright flick. *Friday the 13th*, *Cujo* and *The Evil Dead*, all scared us off the edge of our cinema seats. Donald Pleasance featured in a myriad of such movies, most heavily in *Halloween*. Each time he appeared on screen, one of us always marked the moment by shouting 'Freddie Villiers', on account of his uncanny resemblance to the man who masterfully read the WOS soccer report each Sunday.

But it was the footy that made WOS what it was. In addition to somewhat 'tired and emotional' ex-football heroes arguing the toss over the previous day's play, there was always plenty else worth watching. Umpires were asked to explain themselves during a segment entitled 'What's Your Decision?', which featured footage of unfathomable free kicks awarded in yesterday's games. The highlights for me were the 'Mark of the Day' and 'Goal of the Day' departments.

'Mark of the Day' featured Trevor Barker almost every week. Having seen him in action only twenty-four hours earlier, I was able to anticipate his appearances. St Kilda games were generally given little attention, and in the days before trial by video, many matches were not caught on camera at all. Some of the game's most magnificent marks live only in the memories of those who were there. Of course, this situation offers ample opportunity for exaggeration (which is why so many old people are bullshit artists, there's no evidence!).

Hawthorn rover Leigh Matthews and Geelong winger Michael Turner had a monopoly on 'Goal of the Day' for a number of years. Matthews was a strong mark, but his best goals came from grabbing the ball on the bounce and bulldozing through half a dozen opposition defenders.

Head down, he would spin one way and then the other like a demolition ball on legs, finishing with an accurate snap-shot over his shoulder. One such occasion saw him snap a solid timber point post in half, so pity any poor defender, made of mere skin and bone, who dared stray into his path.

Michael Turner favoured fluency. He liked to run around the boundary line, long hair flowing, bouncing his way towards the goals. Turner was at his best when going the 'big baulk' — that almost extinct skill of holding the ball out wide, away from the body, in one hand, as bait, before suddenly shifting direction like a shoal of fish. Opponents were left floundering in his wake.

'Coaches Corner' was a post-mortem where the previous day's opposing coaches were introduced to the studio audience to the accompaniment of the winning side's theme song. So much for subtlety. For the defeated, it was like a public punishment. Following particularly bad losses, an assistant coach might appear instead, and on some occasions, it was one of the players, usually the team captain, who fronted up to the panel's questioning, shamefaced and fidgety.

St Kilda wins were so scarce that few really begrudged being beaten by our boys. This was how opposition sides and supporters seemed to view a loss to St Kilda. The novelty value was sufficient for them to swallow their pride. I found such an attitude insulting. Patronising. The atmosphere on WOS would be electric after we'd won. Perhaps everyone felt so sorry for us that a rare Saints victory caused general feelings of bonhomie and goodwill. Everybody on the programme bathed in glory on the Saints' behalf. Encourage the underdog.

Without a moped to muck around on or a colour TV to twiddle with, two weeks away from school was a long time. Dad was not a big fan of heading off on holidays. He was a cop and, as far as I know, wasn't on the take, so maybe we couldn't afford to. Mark was always out with his mates, and most of our friends were running around at Rosebud or some similar beachside destination. All that time hanging around the house meant that Simon and I began inventing games.

A favourite was 'Windy Day'. What a game it was! There had to be lots of leaves blowing around outside or a high gale bending the trees in half before the game could be played properly. Facing each other about five paces apart on the front lawn, Simon and I stood very still. Then, on the count of three, we'd start spinning around on the spot, arms in the air, shouting 'windy day, windy day, windy day!', for as long as possible before we were too dizzy to do it any more. We tried the same idea in different conditions, but 'Rainy Day' just didn't have the same ring to it.

Dad being a cop was no big deal. The positive side was easier entry into places when I was with him. The only negative was when a conversation suddenly concluded as I entered a classroom. Kids discussing how they rode their minibikes unlicensed in illegal areas worried about whether I'd dob them in to my Dad. As if!

Another Windy Day-style brainwave saw us spend entire afternoons rolling down hills. On the way to Fats' house, there was a great big, green grassy hill where no houses had been built because of the power-line pylons that ran down the middle. We ran repeatedly to the top of the hill, lay on the ground with our arms out straight above our heads, then rolled and rolled and rolled and rolled all the way to the bottom. It was during this procedure that I discovered there is at least one thing worse than *stepping* in dog shit.

The Tribunal

Monday night tribunal sessions were a worry for supporters who'd seen one of their stars reported on the weekend. If there was an important player or virtually any member of a top team involved, or if the incident being investigated was of particular interest, the media sent a full-scale camera crew to cover the evening's events, with intermittent 'live' crosses and updates. The 'live' cross was a futile attempt at filming rapidly moving footballers fleeing the building, the TV lighting causing blinding white flashes that reflected off elevator doors and closed car windows as the guilty party was whisked away without remark. I wondered whether it was the suspension or the idea of being seen wearing a suit that caused the players to be so coy. If the player involved was of lesser importance, tribunal results would be reported as they came to hand, appearing along the bottom of our TV screens without actually interrupting whatever else we were watching. Often this would be *Cop Shop*, which was on after I was supposed to be in bed. Unless I was allowed a late night, I had to sneak out of my room and watch it on the sly from a kitchen chair. The four or five steps required to find the perfect vantage point took forever as the soles of my feet stuck slightly on the lino floor with each step, making a noise if I wasn't patient. I could see the telly from the kitchen without being visible to anyone in the lounge room. Anyone but not anything. Coco could see from where she sat and sometimes cocked her head in curiosity, alerting Mum and Dad and thus putting an end to my plan.

Prisoner was precious to my Nana. She never missed an episode. Her favourite was Lizzie Birdsworth, the wrinkly one played by Sheila Florence. I often heard Nana from my bedroom at night, singing the theme song as the credits rolled to end yet another instalment, her voice coming through the Vulcan heater air vents which served both ends of the house.

Nana loved singing to herself. With eyes closed and specs off, she'd lean back in the armchair and warble tunes I didn't recognise in an eerie over-the-top operatic style. Her one concession to the sounds of my generation was when she played the Stevie Wonder single *I Just Called To Say I Love You* so many times that the neighbours eventually called to say precisely the opposite.

Nana's singing was sporadically drowned out by ferocious one-way marital arguments, featuring Dad as the bad guy. Mum felt obliged to help keep the local Pinewood shopkeepers in business, a support-your-community kind of thing that bordered on addiction. She enjoyed the village-like atmosphere, driving Dad mad with her constant spending on knick-knacks and magazines. Whenever Dad lost his temper, Mum tended to steer towards tears, leaving the old man 'discussing' the details alone. Standing by the bunks in our darkened bedroom, I committed myself to pluck up the courage required for a confrontation. 'If Dad swears at Mum one more time, I'm going out to say something', I'd announce, in my racing-car pyjamas, with Sim begging me to get back into bed. He needn't have bothered, because, being frozen stiff with fear, I couldn't move a muscle...'

Mum had never seen an episode of *Prisoner*. Her preferred TV programmes were shown while I was at school. The ladies in our street took notes and swapped ideas on what was happening in the American daytime soapies, with *Days of Our Lives* and *The Young and the Restless* being the most popular. Any of the women going away for a while could rest assured there'd be a full, written run-down of events awaiting their return.

One of these women, the bird-like and ultra-efficient Mrs Swift, duly took it upon herself to run a Melbourne Cup sweep for the daytime soapie squad, at fifty cents per person. As this was the only time she gambled, Mum was genuinely excited each year at the prospect of keeping the kitty if her horse won the race, becoming decidedly depressed for a while afterwards when, invariably, it didn't. Her undiluted delight when she finally succeeded, with Black Knight, was a joy to behold. 'Whack-oh! What a bottler!', she cried, as he passed the post first.

CHAPTER NINE

The Family Fun Days

We met a bloke from *Cop Shop* at one of the St Kilda Football Club's Family Fun Days. The Family Fun Day was an annual event filled with fund-raising festivities. Players and Saints-supporting celebrities mixed with ordinary footy supporters. 'J.J.' was a grumpy detective played by Peter Adams in the top-rating police drama series. Our encounter with the actor occurred by accident, literally, when Simon stepped on Adams' small son while running hard for a mark, eyes fixed firmly on the ball. 'J.J.' abused us as he carried the crying boy away. The incident seemed a travesty of the spirit of the day.

I always took both my autograph books to these events. One book was strictly for Saints players, while the other was for anyone else who mattered. In the first book were names such as Grant Thomas, then St Kilda centre half-back, who signed at a 'Slug' Jordan shopping-centre footy show, and Mordecai Bromberg, a ruck-rover and the only Jewish player in the VFL. In the second book appeared the likes of Evonne Goolagong, her signature obtained at the airport when Simon went off to England,

Gus Mercurio, whom I cornered at the annual motor show in the Exhibition Buildings, and Bob Jane of racing car and T-Mart tyre chain fame.

I even once attended a Richmond fund-raising day at Punt Road oval. The event was called the Tetley Tea Party, after their sponsors at the time. Late in the afternoon, some massive bloke grabbed my non-Saints book from renowned rover Barry Rowlings, whom I had asked politely for his autograph, and stuck his own signature in it: 'Barrie Trotter'. I was upset by his audacity, and by the fact I'd never heard of him, though I later learned he was a low number on Richmond's pre-season list. Besides, the way he spelt his first name was a bit suss. Having sullied my precious collection, he proceeded to hand my book to his mates, assuring me they were stars of the senior side. I knew better, but was too scared to say so. Kids no doubt become annoying after a while, and these blokes must've found pissing me off very funny after a few pots.

I wanted to throw the book away after Trotter and his vagrant associates had despoiled and devalued it, but couldn't, because in that same book, on a different page, had been the pen of my cricketing idol, Rodney Hogg, vicious Test fast bowler. It was blasphemy! Nor was ripping a page out an option. I'd tried this in the past and knew that one page out sees the rest follow fast.

Heading home that afternoon, I saw my first dead body. Richmond station stood still for hours due to a corpse underneath a carriage. Simon and I swapped platforms for a better view, but all we could see was a detached hand. We were more fascinated than frightened. Was the death deliberate or accidental, we wondered. Mum had seen it on the news, so we weren't in any trouble for getting back so late. She was happier than ever to see us home safely that night.

Kardinia Park

Kardinia Park was my favourite away ground. We went there in 1981 for the first time, the Richmond station incident having made Mum wary of allowing us to travel too far for a while. The Blue Rattler from Spencer Street station was slightly older than the Red Rattler, but as kids, both trains allowed us to sit in the open doorways during the journey. We arrived at the Geelong ground in time to see Glen Middlemiss kick the last five of his ten goals in the Reserves game. The Reserves won, which we thought was a good omen.

Sporting spiky straw-coloured hair like a scarecrow, Middlemiss had joined St Kilda from Geelong and was one of those players who was far too good for the Reserves yet not quite good enough for a full-time career in the firsts. Mark Scott was another. We signed him from Hawthorn, where he'd kicked more goals at full-forward in the seconds than any other player ever. We didn't realise it was because he'd had so many opportunities to do so. (To be fair, he *was* our leading goal kicker for two seasons and once bagged nine on the great Geoff Southby.)

Towards the end of what became a hundred-point hiding in the main game that afternoon, St Kilda's cheer squad chose to justify their journey to Kardinia Park by treating the place as if it were the local tip. While soccer supporters overseas vented their frustration by kicking the crap out of everybody, we chose to show no mercy and make a mess instead. What must've been fifty phone books were strewn around, each page ripped into quarters. For no apparent reason, I suddenly snatched a section of torn paper as it fluttered past me. Of the thousands of shreds flying about like ticker tape, the piece I had plucked from the air had Trevor Barker's home phone number in Dingley on it. *Dead set!* I considered it an amazing coincidence, and did my own version of *The Twilight Zone* theme music as I showed it to Simon. On the return trip, we gazed open-mouthed at the lights of the oil refineries, flame forever burning, as we clattered past in the darkness.

The Western Oval

The Western Square would be a more appropriate name for the Bulldogs' home ground. Its ends were more right-angled than curved. If we weren't standing behind the goals, we gathered on the Doug Hawkins' wing, opposite the members' stand. The Footscray coaches' box was up a ladder amongst the crowd, enabling us to hurl abuse at the coaching staff as they climbed down at quarter-time. The ladder was just long enough to give us time to finish yelling about how useless the coach was before he reached ground level. That way, he wouldn't be able to identify the loudmouth. Cowardly, I confess, but we didn't need to show courage ourselves. We'd paid our money to see that.

We looked forward to the annual Western Oval afternoon for one reason above any other. The Peanut Man. 'Eeaahh, peanuts!', came the cry as the former porn-shop owner (or so rumour had it) went about selling his peanuts, still in shells, to the punters. He provided the culinary highlight of every season: a fistful of nuts for forty cents, bound in a white-paper bag. He carried them in a huge hessian sack, slung over his shoulder, which must've affected the way he walked even when he wasn't working. We often bought some without even wanting to, just for a laugh. I'd forget, then discover them in my pocket when halfway home on the train. Bonus!

Behind the goals at Footscray's home ground provided as many funny moments as did games at Moorabbin. On one occasion, we watched from under the Simsmetal sign, the Doggies managed a long line of handpasses, creating the loose man and leaving Gary Colling, our full back, in a no-win situation. He attacked the oncoming player, knowing full well that his direct opponent, Steve McPherson, would be the glory boy back in the goal square. McPherson, the lone forward, duly accepted the final handpass. Instead of a toe-tap over the line, he ran hard and hammered the ball into the crowd, hitting some poor old bastard with a beard and a beanie full in the face. Standing with a can in his hand, he'd have done well to get out of the way even if he'd been sober. He wasn't and he didn't. The impact of the footy hitting his head lifted his feet from under him. He hung in midair for a moment, defying gravity, horizontally holding the same position he'd been standing in, then hit the ground like a failed parachutist. Sadly, nobody helped. We were all laughing so hard it hurt our stomachs.

Years before Dr Edelston's Sydney Swans, the Western Suburbs started the showbiz stunts. Footscray always dragged the club mascot, Scragger the bulldog, onto the ground before the game. He'd huff and puff about for five minutes before shuffling back inside. That was it. A week's work done and back on the dog food. What a job. The half-time break saw the Yarraville Brass Band trot out a few tunes. Obesity must have been a prerequisite for band membership, as they were all enormously overweight, not unlike Scragger himself. A blanket carried around the ground raised funds for the cheer squad. Held open by the corners, it became a catching mitt, with helpers picking up inaccurately aimed donations. We threw coins only to see if we could hit someone on the skull. A fifty-cent piece was way too much, but we'd chuck them anyway, because the coin had corners.

I winced one Monday morning, though, when I read on the injury list of Gary Colling's problems. His ailment? 'Lacerated buttocks'. I'd never heard of either word, so asked Dad what it meant, but before he could answer, Mark yelled from the bathroom: 'Sliced-up arse cheeks'. I was horrified. 'Fruit tingles!' I said, which was our school's playground equivalent of 'Fuck Me'.

I was known for never shutting up, which inspired a breakfast table scheme involving an offer of five bucks from my brothers if I could remain mute for five minutes. 'Easy money', I'd say, scraping the burnt surface off my toast and into the sink, as Simon turned down Gavin Wood on the radio. Mark started the clock. Simon would then turn a page in the sports section of the newspaper and express his shock at the report on how Trevor Barker had broken his leg at training. I would immediately demand to be shown the story, losing my chance of winning five bucks. I fell for it every time. I think I'd have rather sacrificed the money than miss out on up-to-the-minute news, just in case the tale was ever true.

In my own defence, I must say that Barker was a regular in the newspapers for both his high-marking skills and his lack of luck in the injury area. He also featured in the social pages more than most, mainly due to his 'way with women'. During his first few seasons, Barker was the boyfriend of Tommy Hafey's daughter, Karen. With Hafey coaching Collingwood, I was always confident of our chances against them. I thought Barker's whole relationship was a ruse to assist us in our matches against the Magpies. It was like having someone on the inside. I imagined Barker having Friday night fish and chips at his girlfriend's house, attempting to extract information from her dad across the kitchen table. Anything he obtained could then be used to our advantage. I began to wonder whether he should try the same trick with other coaches and their kin.

CHAPTER TEN

The Re-enactment

In 1979, Trevor Barker flew above Essendon's Dennis Scanlon to take what officially became the mark of the year, at least according to Channel Seven's *World of Sport* judging panel. The Channel Two football show, *The Winners*, gave their mark of the year award that season to Richmond's Michael Roach for a grab against Hawthorn. But few took much notice of the ABC. Thus, Seven's *World of Sport* 'Mark of the Year' title carried more clout than its Channel Two equivalent, and Seven saw fit to choose Barker as the most brilliant. We were aged nine then, yet twenty years on, this is *still* a source of regular argument among me and my mates.

The Winners was a poor relation when it came to televised footy coverage. The programme's presentation had as much spark as a wet box of matches. Former Essendon ruckman Geoff Leek spoke slow and low, like Bill the Steam Shovel from the *Mr. Squiggle* show, while legendary Essendon hard man Doug Bigelow was so infuriated by the state of modern-day football, he was unable to make a point. He also possessed what was known among the boys at my school as a 'bum' nose, due to its strange split down the centre. Channel Seven's *Football Replay*, by contrast, featured the likes of Lou Richards, Bobby Skilton, Peter Landy and Sandy Roberts, all of whom called the games in an exciting manner, with more cameras, instant replays and live crosses at their disposal. In comparison, *The Winners* looked like amateur hour to a kid with a short concentration span.

So impressed was I with Barker's mark, I decided to recreate the event on our front lawn. My St Kilda scrapbooks contained every article I found anywhere concerning the Saints. Using my red Clag brush, I'd place each item on the page with all the skill and care of a newspaper paste-up artist. A photo of Barker's mark had been printed on the front page of *The Sun* on the Monday morning following his fabulous feat. This photo became my inspiration for the project.

I planned the re-enactment meticulously to ensure success. I needed at least one strong, willing adult, a camera, a roll of film, someone to take the shot and an 'extra' to feature in the photo. Mark and Simon made themselves available, obviously hoping to become a part of history. With the scrapbook open at the appropriate page and set upon the bonnet of the family Hillman Hunter for easy reference, we mirrored Barker's mark *precisely*. I wore my St Kilda Number 1 jumper and Mark teetered about with me balanced high on his back. For added authenticity, we even got Rohan Donnelly (son of the next-door neighbour who'd been on *Don Lane*) to stand nearby, looking on as Scanlon's Essendon teammate had done. Simon snapped away at the result until the film was finished.

I exaggerate a little when using the word 'precisely', because there were just a few discrepancies. For a start, I wasn't Trevor Barker, and Essendon's Dennis Scanlon certainly was not smoking a Marlboro nor wearing Levi jeans and a silver-threaded Miller shirt when Barker landed on his shoulders (unlike Mark, whose lack of an official Bomber outfit slightly marred the moment). That aside, and apart from the Hillman parked in the foreground, it was spot on. It had taken me a week to attempt what my hero had done in a split second. The end result was so impressive that a visually impaired football illiterate may well have mistaken it for the real thing.

Mark at this point was in a band, Horizon. He was the drummer when they appeared on the Channel 0 talent show *Pot of Gold*, hosted by Tommy Hanlon Junior, our family's TV debut! Mark became the lead singer after the show's high-camp critic, Bernard King, accused their female songstress, Kay, of having a 'fat bum'. Despite her brilliant retort ('Are you speaking about a part of me or all of yourself?'), she quit within the week.

Peter Peckham lived on our street, and became a mate of Mark's through hanging around with the band during their rehearsals in our garage. With his top lip a ripe pimple plaza, Peter was a sort of roadie cum wannabe band member with no musical talent but an unfathomable physical affliction: a second arsehole. Definitive details were never provided, but somehow, due to either birth defect or unfortunate accident, Peter's left buttock accommodated a second exit for effluent.

Peter's house had a built-in pool out the back, which we got to use in the summer. Prior to this, we'd created our own waterslides by laying a long sheet of blue plastic out on the lawn with the hose running onto it. Mark spent most of his time in the pool holding my head underwater until I thought I was about to burst. After one such incident, I angrily confronted Mark, simultaneously coughing up chlorine and screaming: 'If you drown me, I'm telling Mum!'.

The Duffle-Coat

The serious footy supporter wore a duffle-coat covered in decorations. The standard practice was to have your favourite player's number sewn on the back, with his Christian name above and his surname below. The lapels were a sea of badges, some sporting individual player's faces and others embarrassingly bad mottoes such as 'I'm A One-Eyed Saints Supporter' or 'Red White & Black Attack'. Onto the sleeves were stitched players' names, sold in separate strips.

During a match at Moorabbin against Essendon, the usual torrential rain forced us up into the grandstand. Squeezing in among a large group of Essendon supporters with pre-booked seats, we watched in silence as the Bombers gave the Saints a belting. At game's end, we were approaching the exit before Simon noticed I wasn't wearing my duffle-coat. I ran back to where we had sat, but the precious coat was nowhere to be seen. Mum was upset, but not half as much as I was.

The duffle-coat wasn't alone in receiving the decorative treatment. My bike, school books, schoolbag and bedroom walls were like shrines to the St Kilda Football Club. Team posters were at the top of the list. Each new season was announced with one, topped by a bold statement in large lettering. 'Saints Alive in '85'! and similar footy-club clichés. Players stood with legs astride, arms folded and fists clenched against the back of the biceps to make muscles look larger. These photo sessions often exposed a sophisticated sense of humour. A pervasive practical joke meant poster release dates were often put back after the printers discovered a player with his penis poking out. Neither Mike Fitzpatrick nor Peter Moore were ever among the accused in such instances.

Windy Hill

In fact, anything to do with Essendon has caused me discomfort in some form. The train from Flinders Street to the Windy Hill ground gradually become a solid chunk of football supporters as Saturday shoppers dispersed in dribs and drabs at each stop along the way, replaced by a tide of team colours.

Tony Morris, our ultra-relaxed cousin from Bendigo, lacked our fervour for footy, so usually saved his visits to Melbourne for the summer. During one rare winter appearance, Tony had little choice but to join us on our

Saturday outing. The fixture dictated that we head for Windy Hill. As usual, the day was a disaster. It rained longer and harder than usual and our team got trounced by more than usual. Apart from questioning why we'd attended at all, Tony later announced his amazement that not once throughout the afternoon had it occurred to Simon and me to go home.

Under Kevin Sheedy's guidance, Essendon was a rugged and ruthless team. Old hands prevailed. Garry Foulds, Merv Neagle, Ronnie Andrews and Roger Merrett, considered 'hard men' by the media, were among the enforcers. Simon insisted that Merrett was the spitting image of the Paddle Pop lion. Whenever he went near the ball, my brother shouted: 'Paddle Pop!', to the complete bewilderment of all around us.

The journey home took forever. Fortunately, Simon and I knew every word to each team's theme song. I didn't know my nine times table, but I can still sing *Sons of the 'Scray* all the way through. Every so often, we'd go through the lot for a laugh, maybe on the train home from a game or when riding about aimlessly on our bikes.

I had long believed that the team theme songs were sung to original tunes. I wasn't aware that most had new lyrics set to well-known musical standards. *The Marseillaise*, for example. Until this fact dawned on me, I could never work out why, on the international news, French President Charles de Gaulle was always being greeted by bands belting out *We are the Boys from Old Fitzroy*.

As I grew older and began attending eighteenth-birthday parties, an ensemble rendition of footy club theme songs usually signified that the evening was entering its last hour. It also served as a tribal display of grief at the beer running out.

CHAPTER ELEVEN

The Real Thing

Down the players' race we ran, onto the MCG. Exhilaration. This was to be the most important game of our lives. The weeks leading up to it had been a barrage of team meetings, extra training sessions and even tears, as players were slowly but surely informed of their selection chances. Richmond versus Melbourne. The Little League. Our school was fortunate enough to be selected, and the opportunity gave me added zip. I made the side.

I struggled to sleep the night before, with ideas of taking the spekky of the century and being signed up on the spot racing through my mind. The rules allowed something like thirty players per team to participate, so our school decided to swap everyone at half-time — except the goal-to-goal line, the spine of the side. We wanted to win after all. The goal-to-goal line got a full game, and as full back, I featured in the entire twenty minutes. Both ten-minute halves.

Wayne Bulte, the kid with same birthday as Trevor Barker, was our full forward. His dad promised him a dollar a goal, fifty cents a point. Wayne played very well and made himself two bucks, despite going goalless. Back then, the ground wasn't reduced in size for the little runts, so changing ends at half-time meant ten-year-old legs running the full length of the MCG.

My opponent was a chubby full forward. The play was way down the other end. We were trouncing them. I desperately wanted to leave the goal square, in the hope of getting a kick, so I tried talking him into moving downfield, towards the action. 'Go on then', he said, standing steadfast, arms crossed across his chubby-bubby boobs, 'but if the ball comes down to me and I get a goal, it won't look good for the full back, will it?'.

Being the full back, it was just what I didn't want to hear. The Richmond cheer squad was chanting: 'Meatloaf', clap, clap, clap, 'meatloaf' in his direction, even though he was representing their own side. He was not going to budge, so I accepted my fate and, as a result, failed to record a single statistic. So much for the spekky of the century. There is no visual record of my involvement in that match anyway, due to my refusal to be photographed wearing a Melbourne jumper.

We joined our families soon afterwards in the specially allocated seats to see Bruce Monteath kick eight goals in the main game. Later that year, the Tigers won the flag and as captain, Monteath sat on the bench almost all day. Another bloke called Daryl Freame was picked in that grand final team, yet didn't so much as set foot on the hallowed soil. He spent the entire match on the bench and never played for Richmond again. So while it was a fact that I'd not got a kick, at least by getting onto the ground, I was one up on *somebody*.

My First Flight

I generally stuck to the same solid stable of regular friends, though others drifted in and out. Each new year saw a new class of different kids, and the occasional new friend was like a fad. Michael and I fitted this description for each other in Grade Four. He had bright-red hair and thick-rimmed glasses and he liked to eat his scabs, but otherwise he was okay. We must've been friends for six months before I hit the jackpot. His birthday was upon us and his parents promised him a plane flight as a present. He was also allowed to bring a friend along. Eureka!

When it came to all-time ambitions, the chance to fly in a plane was right up there with a day in Disneyland and was not very far behind St Kilda winning the flag or Trevor Barker winning the Brownlow. I was so excited, I accepted his invitation immediately, even though we'd be setting off on a Saturday morning and may not be back in time for the match. I had no idea that in the week before the flight, St Kilda would sack Mike Patterson and employ Alex Jesaulenko as coach. Playing coach, to add icing to the cake.

It was unbelievable. Two games into the season and still without a win, the arrival of Jesaulenko was huge for St Kilda. How could I miss this match? Is there anything more thrilling than a team's first game under a new coach, especially mid-season. Supporters always convince themselves that a new broom sweeps clean, forgetting about the team performances that saw the old coach sacked in the first place. Regarded then as perhaps the game's greatest player, and fresh from winning the flag as captain-coach of Carlton, Jesaulenko was a master, and we waited anxiously for him to weave his wizardry. The game was to be against Richmond at the MCG, but I decided to stick to the original agreement. I'd lost some sleep, but looked forward to seeing the suburbs from high in the sky.

Saturday came and we were up, up and away. I experienced no fears or phobias and the flight was even more fun than I'd imagined. I have a photo of me and Michael standing beside the Fokker Friendship. Michael is resplendent in jumper and jeans. I'm wearing St Kilda socks, shorts and shirt.

We arrived home and ran around the block together to tell my parents everything. Turning the corner into my street, I saw my brother in the back of a car with his mate Clutch, a Tigers supporter whose mum was taking them to the train station. I wanted to go along too, but Mum wouldn't let me. Michael didn't follow the football much, so if I'd gone to the match, he would have been left alone, she insisted. Was I was prepared to forget about my friend on his birthday, push him into the background only hours after enjoying a free plane flight, all because an ex-Carlton player had become

St Kilda coach? Well, yes I was, actually, but wasn't given the chance.

The game was a draw. We listened on the radio, the tension almost making me explode. I wanted to hit my mate for making me miss it. I wonder what would've happened if we'd won. Michael and I drifted apart after that. My selfishness regarding St Kilda had no limits. I was lost in a football frenzy.

The last game of that same season was a draw against North Melbourne at Arden Street, which was significant not just for being St Kilda's second draw in the one season but also because it meant we narrowly avoided yet another wooden spoon, an area in which we led by an embarrassing margin. Players and supporters alike reacted as if we'd won the flag. We knew enough to be thankful for small mercies.

Clutch fascinated us with his ability to remain emotionless when watching his beloved Tigers. Perhaps his Swedish heritage explained his cool head in all situations. Through tight scores, great goals and outrageous umpiring decisions, Clutch was tight-lipped, whereas in similar situations involving the Saints, Simon and I came close to having actual heart attacks. We couldn't even go to a game in which St Kilda wasn't playing without gradually beginning to support one side or the other. What was the point, after all?

The draw with Richmond was one thing, but we wanted a win. St Kilda's second game under the great man's guidance saw a successful wave of his wand — we scraped home against Essendon, finalists the previous season. The triumph was somewhat overshadowed, though, by 'Fabulous' Phil Carman's classic contribution, which kicked off when he whacked Garry Sidebottom and concluded when he head-butted the boundary umpire. He eventually copped twenty weeks for his work. This all took place in front of our spot behind the goals, but as the entire fracas was by the fence, I couldn't see a thing for all the heads in the way. So despite having been present at possibly the most unruly incident to have taken place in a game of senior League football, my memories of the event are restricted to footage from the *Sensational Seventies* video, like everybody else.

As for the first win under our new Messiah, the Saints' revival was short-lived. We were thrashed over the following five weeks and won only three more games that season. For Sidebottom, a strong, exciting centre half-forward from Swan Districts in Western Australia, the event marked the beginning of the end with St Kilda. Later in the year, he fell to the ground on the members' wing at Moorabbin, apparently the victim of a beer can in the face. Aside from the upset caused by the actual throwing of the can, news film showed it missing 'Sidey' by a mile, making him the subject of general derision for having taken a dive.

The signing of Jezza saw crowds increase at Moorabbin, our own parents being among the converted. An action shot in *The Sunday Press* of the tinnie soaring towards Sidebottom showed Mum and

Dad in the crowd — Mum instantly recognisable by her Elton John-style sunglasses — with Simon, who had found Mum to ask for money to buy a pie, alongside them. (We stood apart from our parents whenever they came to a game so that we could swear at the umpire unhindered.) As keeper of the cuttings, I was far from happy to have been absent from the shot. I could have been in my own scrapbook! Sidebottom joined Geelong the next season.

The Men In White

Simon was one of the rare characters who acknowledged early and apparently without regret that a senior game with the Saints was beyond his abilities. Still footy-mad, and at an age where the careers lady at school wanted an answer, Simon pushed aside the constant, inexplicable offers of French-polishing apprenticeships and asked about an advertisement for umpires he'd spotted in the 'Employment' pages.

Dad drove Sim to a mass meeting for people interested in the profession, and together they were witness to what was a particularly sorry state of affairs. The meeting consisted of one bitter old suburban-league umpire after another speaking to the assembled throng about The Job. Instead of encouraging those with questions or otherwise motivating potential workmates, each speaker used the opportunity to tell some story about how he'd 'got his own back' on footballers who'd fooled them at some point in the past. Simon left before the last bloke had finished, having confirmed the belief we supporters held in the stands — umpires are offal. He was embarrassed, in hindsight, that he'd even considered sleeping with the enemy. What had he been thinking?

Players aren't the only ones trying to 'put one over' the umpires. If circumstances are on its side, a crowd at any given game is able to affect the outcome of many situations on the field. Granted, there are genuine mistakes made when umpires need to make line-ball decisions, but I can recall games where we influenced those decisions in our team's favour. In the case of a Saints player shooting for goal at Moorabbin, the crowd behind the posts often reacted to a narrow miss by cheering wildly, as if for a goal, in case the goal umpire wasn't too sure. We assisted the Saints to several goals over the years with such dishonest applause. If an opposition player kicked accurately, on the other hand, we'd go delirious with derisory delight at his 'miss', hoping the goal umpire might be deceived into seeing the matter our way. Intriguingly, these falsified mass reactions were never organised in advance; they just happened, each of us hoping we could help our boys out somehow, by fair means or foul.

In any case, we believed that foul means were often employed by the umpires to 'even up' the free-kick ratio towards the end of a game. As keen as the next person to keep their jobs, the umpires obviously had as much access to updated statistics at each break as did the media. Therefore, if one team had received many more free kicks than the other by, say, half-time or three-quarter time, we felt that the umpires would be doing their damnedest to balance the ledger by game's end, thus avoiding the wrath of their boss, be it Harry Beitzel, Bill Deller or whoever else led the umpires' governing body at the time.

CHAPTER TWELVE

The Under 14s

The Little League whetted the footy appetite, and it wasn't long before I was turning out for a real team: the Nottinghill B side. They wore blue and white vertical stripes, like North Melbourne. Someone had heard they were struggling to field a full team, and during one particularly laborious science lesson, a few of us decided to sign up together. The ground was near to where we all lived and training was every Tuesday and Thursday after school. The A side trained at the same time and place, but on a different area of the oval.

Every so often, the coach of the A team would ask one of our group to join in with them. I thought I'd rather play with my mates in the Bs, but secretly hoped they'd haul me over to the As one day. I was never given the choice. The one benefit was; the As played on Saturday mornings, whereas the Bs played on Sunday afternoons. In the Bs, I wouldn't miss seeing the Saints play anywhere *and* I could sleep late on the weekend.

We finished training in time to be home for tea. Running home on a Thursday night, the streetlights reflecting off slick, wet roads and my breath creating icy clouds in front of my face, I stuck to the nature strips, hurdling concrete driveways so that I wouldn't wear down my stops. Under our outside porch light, I bashed my boots against the front step (the dirt came off in thick layers, with see-through circles where the stops had been, like mini biscuit moulds) before coming inside to eat the steak I could smell cooking.

Mum insisted on buying me a mouth-guard. The properly fitted jobs were worth a fortune, so we returned from the chemist with a clear-plastic horseshoe instead. One size fits all. The instructions stated that it should be boiled in hot water before being bitten into, so it would mould itself into the shape of my mouth. The taste and texture of the hot, gummy plastic was putrid. Worse than Brussels sprouts.

We were the least talented team of junior footballers ever to have pulled on a pair of poorly fitted moulded soles. On the surface, it appeared we could play, but the fact was that we never won. No, we lost. Often. By massive margins. A team called Knox once kicked forty-five goals against us on our home ground! Opposition coaches had an unfortunate habit of swapping their entire forward line with the back line at three-quarter time, to give everybody a chance to kick goals. Luckily, our coach never tried a similar ploy, or we'd all have had the chance to get a goal kicked against us. Not that he needed to. It happened anyway. Our full forward had goals kicked against him on more than one occasion, the other team's full back simply fleeing up the field with no fear of embarrassment. Meanwhile, our forward line, having given up hope of handling the ball before the game even started, involved themselves in mud fights to fend off the freezing cold.

Sliding around in the slop was sometimes enough fun in itself. Wearing rubber bands (or the sliced-off ends of dishwashing gloves) as garters kept my footy socks up, though they also cut off the circulation in my lower legs. Giving the garters a miss, though, meant masses of mud soaking into my socks, which then fell down around the ankles, making each foot seem to weigh five stone.

On my feet were a pair of adidas 'Leeds' footy boots. They had moulded soles, because screw-ins were too expensive and also because the places where each stop was positioned hurt the sole of my foot like hell. I learnt that just from walking around the shop wearing a pair. Kids who wore them said the same thing. All the same, I dreamed of stepping onto the field one day in adidas 'Valencias', with the fluorescent green stripes and matching sole. They were screw-ins, but as I'd always been addicted to anything glow-in-the-dark, I would gladly have put up with the pain.

Our pre-game preparations were preposterous. We rubbed liniment on ourselves for no other reason than that's what the real players did. Some kids wrapped Elastoplast around their wrists, without any actual need for it. Trainers shook resin on our hands from battered alloy tins like the salt shakers from the fish and chip shop. Intended to improve our grip, this substance appeared to consist of a mixture of parmesan cheese and sand. Before running out, we'd stand facing each other in two horizontal lines, ten kids each, handballing half a dozen footies rapid-fire in all directions. The whole exercise accompanied by the clapping of hands and the yelling out of clichés aplenty: 'C'mon, fire up!', 'We can win this easy' and 'We're better than this bunch of girls'.

Then the stretching started. We paired off and stood back to back, linking arms behind ourselves. Taking turns, we then lifted our partner by bending over, bringing the other kid up off the ground. (I'm still wondering about the point of that one.) Finally, we did ten tuck jumps as a team, counting them out loud. Sometimes, the warm-ups were so rugged that we were stuffed before the game even started.

It was during these warm-ups that the umpires always entered the dressing rooms to check our boot studs for spikes. Apparently, someone, somewhere, at some time in the distant past, had deliberately hammered nails through the bottom of their boots and caused horrible injuries, so umpires running fingers along footballers boots became an important process from that day forward. I wondered whether the 'spike search' was carried out at League level. If not, it sure might explain Gary Colling's lacerated buttocks.

Following a rousing speech by the coach, consisting of comments like 'man up', 'in front', 'eyes on the ball' and 'up the guts', we had one last nervous wee before making a mean face and filing out the door all together, boots clattering on the concrete between the changing-room door and the oval itself.

On-field injuries prompted all manner of amateur diagnosis. 'How many fingers am I holding up?' asked someone's uncle wearing a yellow armband, in cases of possible concussion. Warm flannels or the magic spray cured any other ailments. It's a wonder the impaired players' mothers weren't invited onto the field to rub the injured player's forehead until he fell asleep.

Fats was our full back. Yes, this was the same bloke who couldn't climb fences. At footy training, I avoided him when it came to the back-to-back lifting exercises. We thought he was a fabulous footballer, but to be fair, playing in his possie on our team, he saw more of the ball than the rest of us. Alongside a barrage of goals being booted against us were a fair few points, each one requiring a kick-out from the full back. This was where Fats was our surprise package. Despite dodgy knees incurred as a result of crashing his beloved BMX too many times, Fats dispensed with the standard style of 'going long'. Instead, he'd kick the ball to himself inside the goal square (as was the trend at the time) and go rampaging like a rhino down the centre of the ground, treating opponents much as a bowling ball treats ten pins. After four or five bounces, he'd launch the ball deep into our forward line, then attempt to beat the ball back on its inevitable rapid return to the opposition scoring zone. Once the opposition cottoned onto this solitary attacking tactic, all we had left was Plan B. This involved Fats kicking the ball a short distance to his fast-leading mate in the back pocket — me. In this case, each behind scored by the other side ensured we both got a kick, which was a rarity within our team. Fats was able to get a kick on his own, but Plan B became my best chance of gathering a statistic. My match totals could usually be tallied on one hand. Still, that never deterred me from checking the *Waverley Gazette* each Wednesday to see if I'd been named among the best players. The effort usually proved fruitless. Fats got a regular mention, the typist regularly struggling with the spelling of his name: Tony Khachadourian. The original BMX bandit, Fats could have pulled mono-wheels for Australia. He was content to ride around on his back wheel for whole days at a time, determining the distance of each effort by how many times he peddled before the front wheel returned to the road.

Fats' BMX addiction certainly deprived his dog of its fair share of attention. 'Lucky' was anything but. Sick of waiting to be taken for a walk, the creature followed its own exercise regime in the back yard. For years, it trod the steps of an elaborately formed figure of eight, which was worn about six inches deep. The sight of this psychologically shattered Scottish terrier continually completing this circuit of its own invention, legs invisible below ground level, was bizarre, like some hybrid of shooting-gallery duck and Scalectrix set.

The McDonalds hamburger bosses sent free food vouchers to the local junior football leagues. They were handed out by the coach to whoever played well that week.

Over the years, I cost the corporation no more than a couple of cheeseburgers. We were fortunate in that our ruck-rover and centre half-forward were of certified A-side standard, but were forced by their Saturday morning supermarket shifts to play on a Sunday, thus strengthening our team and taking around ten goals off our inevitable losing margin.

We did have some other outstanding players. It was just that they stood out for all the wrong reasons. Take Phillip Franklynstein, for example. Phillip Franklynstein was, without doubt, the worst footballer I have ever seen at any level. He never missed training and always tried his hardest. He even had specialist help from a skills coach, usually somebody's dad with spare time up his sleeve. Phillip Franklynstein was not disabled in any way, but his feet, head and hands were developing faster than the rest of his physique. He looked like a marionette when going for a mark. The messages from his mind seemed to get lost somewhere between his brain and his limbs. Time and space eluded him. His gauges were gone. He once led out for a mark and, as the footy headed straight for him, either forgot or failed to close his hands around the ball, so that when it hit his chest, with his arms still stuck straight out in front of his body, his face portrayed a state of pure shock, as if he were the victim of some optical illusion.

Phillip and his loyal father, who was forever following his son's fortunes, were friendly, fair-dinkum fellas, but there was no way around the fact that Phillip was a shocking player. Foregoing any argument over moulded sole or screw-in, he played in a pair of K-Mart 'Winners', brown with a beige stripe and resembling Dunlop Volley runners with slightly protruding 'grips' cast into the plastic base. Phillip never got any better, but as we were short on numbers, he always got a game. Surprisingly, for all his flaws, we always offered him our support and never singled him out. Not even for his name.

Jason was big, broad and prepared to back into a pack. He could take a strong mark in the goal square, but that's when the trouble started. Lining up for a shot, his confidence would dissipate. Even when he was dead in front and a few feet out, his mind appeared to melt. No amount of encouragement worked. Eventually, he resorted to faking an injury whenever he took a mark, allowing somebody else to take the kick. He'd bend over in apparent agony, surrounded by assistance, only to straighten up and jump with joy as soon as he heard the sounds of celebration. It was patently ridiculous, but it appeared the ploy was later practised in St Kilda's senior side during Stewart Loewe's first few seasons.

Whilst gaining possession was the main problem, the Nottingham B team's sense of direction was even worse. Andrew, who played in the centre, was a confused type of character. He operated on his own wavelength. Among the few of us who knew how to get the ball, Andrew found changing ends a challenge, often forgetting to kick in the opposite direction after each break. As the ball was bounced to start a new quarter, Andrew would come ducking and weaving out of the centre square, oblivious to our desperate calls, and send the ball soaring towards the other team's end. Realising his mistake, he'd theatrically stomp around in a circle, slapping himself in the head. Moments later, when he grabbed the footy once again, he'd proceed to commit exactly the same crime. If it weren't for his pair of Peter Knights Pumas, we may well have hated him.

Our captain, Ian, known as 'Dillan' for reasons no-one can recall, was a tall, rangy winger with almost-red hair and a largish pair of ears. If our team was a disastrously drought-stricken cattle-ranch, then he was the landowner who was waiting just a little longer before deciding to shoot his stock. Proud. Stoic. Australian. I liked him for a number of reasons, the main one being that he had a ping-pong table at his house. Dillan's finest hour, as the first player to reach fifty games for the Nottinghill Bs, was tarnished somewhat when the doorway-sized banner (made of interwoven vertical and horizontal crêpe-paper strips held together too tightly with standard sticky-tape) almost decapitated him as he tried to lead the team through it. We tried to stifle our amusement while he tearfully played the first half with a red ring round his neck, as if he'd had a lucky escape from the noose.

When he and I were very young, Dill had once accidentally walked in on Mum while she was having a bath. Lying there wearing nothing but a flannel over her eyes, she assumed him to be me and asked him to pass her the Radox . On returning to my room, his whole head was a purpley-red colour and he wouldn't say a word. Later that day, Mum and I worked out what had happened, and though she was a bit embarrassed, we laughed until there were tears rolling down our cheeks.

Most kids' families became involved with the club to some extent. In my case, Simon agreed to be the runner, Mum joined the jumper-washing roster and Dad drove us to the games. Dad was of a high enough rank in the force to be allocated a police car as a private vehicle. As was the case at most local grounds, cars parked around the boundary line, providing people with a seat and good shelter. Dad's cop car had a megaphone mounted on the roof, between the two blue lights, and Dad would use this to offer encouragement during matches. 'Carrrna Hills!', he would blare in booming baritone, totally bewildering the opposition players and sending Fats into such uncontrollable fits of laughter that he couldn't play properly. Dad had to make sure he hollered when the ball was as far away from Fats as possible. If we scored a goal, Dad would sound the siren. I was proud of him and slightly ashamed, all at the same time.

Deep in faraway Ferntree Gully stood a ground named The Basin. Set in the side of a hollowed-out hill, it was colder than an Esky in the Antarctic. At half-time, an assistant would organise a bucket of boiling hot water, into which the players would tentatively dip their fingers in an effort to avoid frostbite. One freezing afternoon, unable to feel my hands anyhow, I shoved them into the bucket and instantly felt all the blood in my body rush to my fingertips. Screaming in pain, I pulled my hands away to see my digits looking like overcooked sizzling sausages about to burst. That was the last of me for the match. I had learned an important lesson: never play football at The Basin.

I never had a shower at the ground after the game. If there were any showers at all, they were teeth-chattering cold with zero pressure. More importantly, I didn't want anyone to discover that I didn't have a very big dick. Logic is lacking when you're fourteen years old with not much of an old fella. I didn't realise the temperature would have seen everyone all shrunken up no matter what their size. Besides, Dad had got us into the St Kilda dressing rooms at Waverley Park one afternoon and some of those blokes were hung like draughthorses. Dean Herbert, a lanky sort signed by the Saints from Sandringham, even had a *Playboy* bunny tattooed just above his prick.

Combined with my willy worries was a fear of anyone setting eyes on my skinny frame. 'You'll fill out. You're just a Slim Jim, that's all', Mum said whenever I started on the subject. Our family doctor, Dr Vasta, a gentle, heavy-lidded greyhound owner who seemed to speak in slow motion, refused to give me any medication to enhance my appetite, so I had to make do with wearing long sleeves or extra layers everywhere. I failed to realise that wearing a windcheater in thirty-degree heat at the Waverley Pool probably attracted more attention than sitting around in my board-shorts.

Some of us wondered how it might feel to have a fight on the field, but we weren't certain how to start one.

Baiting your mates was easy. You knew how to upset them because you knew their insecurities. Comments on the size of your mate's mum's feet, the sour-milk smell given off by his sister or the pair of burgundy cords he has been seen to wear could be relied on to incite swinging fists. Strangers were a different story. Physically, amongst each other, we also had some idea how each opponent could handle himself. No-one wanted to throw the first punch at somebody new.

It happened during a game against Glen Waverley Rovers, whose jumper was just like Collingwood's. They were long-standing flag winners in all divisions, with a renowned full forward named Mark Mercedes. An A-side superstar, Mercedes had the square-jawed good looks of a Nordic horseman and the shifty eyes of a high-stakes poker player. He was as tough as he was talented. Competition rules allowed anybody to play at either A or B level, but not both on the same weekend. When we learned Mercedes would be lining up against us one Sunday afternoon, having missed the previous day's A-side game due to a family function, our coach realised there was only one answer. Violence.

The Coach

Rex, who coached the side for several seasons, was a truck driver with old-fashioned ideas. His son was among my team mates. Rufus was a local hard man and, like his father, had a Fred Flintstone physique. Apart from living in the same street, going to the same school and playing for the same team, Rufus and I had something else in common: we despised each other. I've never known why.

Rufus and I had been students at Syndal Tech for just three days before our first fight. We were in the big league now, so it seemed sensible to seek supremacy from the start, a typically tenuous basis upon which to begin belting each other. A lunchtime kick-to-kick began, involving a big group of boys, with Rufus and I at opposite ends. I began to dominate my end, taking one strong spekky after another. This rare fine form and the ensuing acclaim obviously provoked Rufus' envy, so he swapped ends to make sure it stopped. Intimidated by his bulk, but never one to back down, I took him on. Two more big grabs and I met a smack in the mouth. It was on. Mud. Blood. The works.

Unfortunately, the fight occurred right outside the principal's office, which looked out onto the main oval. We were both beckoned inside. Mr Irvine had an Irish accent, fiery eyes and elf-like facial features. He also had a weird beard, which led us to christen him 'Captain Kremen', after the character on *The Kenny Everett Video Show*. In the time it took for us to wipe the blood from our faces in his foyer, he'd made a few phone calls and found we'd been arch foes for a fair few years, clashing regularly at Pinewood Primary and, on one occasion, at football training.

The strap was still in season at that stage, and it took no more than a brief demonstration of a doubled-up leather belt whacking his desk with a deafening crack, to encourage us to bury our differences. If we couldn't be friends, we should leave each other alone, he said. If not, well, there wouldn't be a second warning.

So, Mark Mercedes the great goal-kicker, runs out for Glen Waverley Rovers in the crappy Collingwood-style black and white stripes. Taking his place at full forward, he had a right to feel confident, playing as he was a level below the one he was used to, against a team with less natural talent than a failed *New Faces* contestant. A tactical mastermind, our coach had devised a cunning plan in which Rufus and I would bury our differences and join forces to defeat the opposition danger-man: we were to bash him up.

Mercedes was part of a pack in the goal square when we got him. Into time-on in the second quarter, he'd already kicked seven. Rising yet again like an ascending Adonis above his flat-footed opponents, he fumbled the first grab and fell groundwards, grasping for a second bite at the cherry. With fingers outstretched, mouth open in anticipation and eyes set firmly on the ball, he was never going to see Rufus unload a lip-splitting left-hander. Mercedes hit the deck, the pack closed around him and, as he lay momentarily exposed, I delivered a deadly knee-drop to the guts. He was a cool dude and a big bloke, but he cried like a baby. The half-time siren sounded, and as we ran towards the dressing room, everybody booed us. I felt like a bad guy. It was brilliant!

Andy Colliss was Rufus's best friend. How Rufus *had* any friends when he insisted on wearing old-fashioned

Ronald Dale Barassi boots that came up over the ankle is beyond me. However, tall, blond, solid and an A-side staple, Andy could do the Rubik's cube in record time. One season, Andy was absent for several weeks. Then, one evening, his mum turned up at training and spoke to the coach. We watched them deep in discussion and could only wonder what had happened. As she walked back to her car, someone asked where Andy was and whether we'd be seeing him again. 'Andy's got no time for football, no time for girls. He's studying to be a doctor', she replied, climbing into her car. We thought this the most hilarious thing we'd ever heard. It was so hilarious, in fact, that we ran around repeating it like a mantra in the twilight during the training session's standard final four laps. 'No time for football, no time for girls.' We found the concept ridiculous. Then again, Andy became a doctor and none of us played professional football.

Unable to coach us for six weeks mid-season, due to a long-distance truck-driving job, Rex was replaced for that period by a fella whose face was fixed in some kind of ghastly grimace, as if permanently reacting to stinging antiseptic on an open wound. Kenny must've been about twenty-five, with allergies or eczema afflicting him in a major way. With his wet lips and tight, white head of closely cropped hair, Kenny coached us in a state of fist-clenching frustration, often incurring the wrath of the umpire for audible abuse from the boundary line.

Two weeks into his tenure, Kenny, who had won us over immediately with his way of treating us as equals, turned up to training with an old, wrinkled, grey-haired woman in his car. She waited in the passenger seat throughout the session, and as we were finishing, Cameron, our deputy vice-captain, asked: 'Hey Kenny, aren't you gonna introduce us to your mum?' Kenny was incredulous. '*Me mum?* Whadya mean, *me mum*? That's me girlfriend!'

Kenny wasn't one of these win-at-all-cost kids' coaches who fails to put things in perspective. He was like the boxing fan who can't watch a fight without riding every punch. If one of us was about to be flattened, he'd twist and turn beforehand as if it were he in the path of the oncoming bump. Then he'd react in agony as if it were he who had received it. Not one to give up easily, Kenny would implore us to improve our performance as if his own life depended on it. For all his frustration and umpire abuse, Kenny always tried to find positive points about our play, and never swore in our company, though we often saw him struggle to stop himself. During his sixth and final game in charge, without a win, we'd squandered an early three-goal lead and were eight goals behind by half-time. The dressing-room atmosphere was ugly. Kenny's well of constructive criticism had finally run dry. 'I tell you what', he said with a sigh after a long pause, 'I'd rather be at home, fucking my girlfriend, than coaching you kids'. There was a shocked silence. This was serious. We'd seen his girlfriend.

Rex returned and Kenny went back to wherever he came from. I hope he had *some* good memories of our team, though I struggle to recall a genuine highlight. At the end of every Nottinghill season came the 'Best and Fairest Awards' night. The club officials would set up a screen and show Super–8 film of footballers in fine form. When it came to winning awards, I was aware that the 'Best and Fairest' was beyond me, but no matter how poorly I'd played throughout the season, I always genuinely believed there was a chance my name would be engraved on the 'Most Consistent' trophy. It never was. Still, my desperate logic had me convinced that while I was not the best player each (or any) week, I also wasn't the worst, which surely counted as consistent.

One day my bus passed a trophy shop and it dawned on me that I could save a lot of time and effort by purchasing my own trophy to stick on the shelf. Unfortunately, I'd also have to move away from my family and friends, who knew the facts.

I was a good 'talker' on the field, though there wasn't an award for this particular skill. I'm not sure if it was genuine enthusiasm or an attempt to pretend I was playing a part in proceedings, but I was always first with the warning, 'You're hot, you're hot', to a team-mate about to be tackled or, 'You're clear, you're clear', whenever a fellow player had the ball in an opponent-free zone. Unfortunately, my cumbersome, cut-price mouth-guard stopped anyone understanding a word I said anyway. I was also good at shouting, 'Touched!' whenever the opposition scored a goal, no matter where I was on the field at the time. When standing on the mark of an opposition player lining up for goal, I timed my standard statement of distraction to the second. 'Fuzz!', I'd suggest sportingly, mouthguard in hand and half-time orange still stuck in my teeth.

My most obvious ability, if I may say so myself, was tackling a player who was 'hatching' the ball, seconds before the umpire blew his whistle for a ball-up. I'd run in at the last moment, pull at his jumper with one hand and hold the other arm in the air, appealing for a free kick. 'He's holding it!', I'd cry, pretending I'd applied the perfect tackle, though more often the other player had merely fallen over on the ball and was too buggered to get up.

My greatest moment in a match came as a result of downright dishonesty. It was a definitive case of shirking the issue. In a game against Mount Waverley, my immediate opponent had kicked three goals within ten minutes of the opening bounce. A resting rover, the little bastard was running rings around me. I reacted by taking the only option available — I faked an injury. Grabbing the area where I imagined my hamstring to be, I dragged the afflicted leg behind me, screaming in 'agonised' imitation of proper League players suffering the same fate. After a quarter on the bench 'recovering', the resting rover had been contained. We were rapidly reducing their lead, but with two genuine injuries, the team was a man short. In a fine example of the Nottingham B attitude, I was sent to full forward *for a rest.*

I was so excited about getting a spell up front that I barely remembered to limp as I made my way onto the ground. The next few minutes saw us score two goals and, by crikey, we were back in the game. Five points behind with a couple of minutes on the clock, I'd yet to have a touch. As I stood in the goal square, the ball arced towards me. I was at the back of the pack when it arrived, hit hands and finally went to ground, dead in front of my right foot. As I swung the boot and heard the siren sound, I realised we had won. I'd kicked the winning goal! Despite furious opposition claims of 'foot through', the goal umpire (our captain's big brother) waved the two white flags.

But prior to my effort was one that mattered more. One of our forwards was pushed in the back and awarded a much-deserved shot at goal. His pitiful kick from not far out, on the easiest of angles, went through for a point, but he was ridden roughly to the ground as the ball passed the posts and was given a second go. He made no mistake, and while goals are always great, this was a magic moment. That night, sitting with his loyal father in the famous fast-food restaurant, Phillip Franklynstein ate free fries. I felt the McDonalds voucher had gone to an even greater act of valour than my own.

CHAPTER THIRTEEN

No Time For Girls

Mrs Colliss claimed her son had 'no time for girls'. Wrong! We *all* had time for girls. The truth was, none of them had any time for us. Cyndi Lauper was lying. The best four or five 'A' players knew the ways of women, as is the fickle hand of fate. Not content to play better than their pals, they also managed to get the girls. The rest of us had absolutely no idea what to say, what to do, where, when, how, or to whom. I, for one, was definitely interested, despite my appalling sexual ignorance. I became aroused when checking out Charlie's Angels and I desperately wanted Sheridan Jobbins, the dark-haired one with the big bazookas on *Simon Townsend's Wonder World*. On my wall was a full-colour 'Big M girl' calendar.

Still, my interest was fleeting. Unless a girl could give me a mint-condition Alle de Wolde, my concentration would probably have wandered anyway. Besides, Sim had started seeing a woman and was gradually paying me less attention than I was used to. I could tell girls were trouble, so I stuck to footy training. Not that I had an option.

Well there *was* Samantha Donnelly, the daughter of the bloke who'd been on the *Don Lane Show*. She was my age and went to my school. With her long, golden hair, fresh face and melting-chocolate way of moving, Samantha looked forever like a mermaid in the sunshine. We played together as kids and got along fine as teenagers, yet so distracted was I by the Saints that I never once attempted anything untowards — either before or after I knew better. There was no showing of mine or yours, no doctors and nurses, no spinning of bottles. I wasn't shy or scared in any way and whether she'd have been willing is beside the point. It simply didn't enter my mind. As an adult, this is a memory I still struggle to comprehend. Had St Kilda been winning flags at that stage, my preoccupation with them might make sense in hindsight. Yet the Saints were shit and still I wouldn't waver.

As Mark grew older, I made a tidy profit from his Sunday morning hangovers by sneaking into his room to collect the coins that scattered across the floor when his hastily discarded dacks hit the deck. I moved in a slow, stilted motion as if illuminated by a strobe light, praying he wouldn't wake up. Not until many years afterwards, when I discovered alcohol myself, did I realise a full-scale marching band wouldn't have woken him after seventeen scotch and cokes. As for my fear of him missing the money, now that I know how hard it is to account for anything up to a hundred bucks after a serious session on the sauce, I feel a fool for thinking he might've noticed five-fifty in loose change.

Simon and I slept in bunk beds until long after he was eighteen. Our original single beds had been arranged one atop the other, to create more floor space. When Mark left home, it created an available room, but Sim chose to remain with me. He was used to the company. When I was about fourteen, he began working. Pay nights, he was usually pissed. I'd wake up around two o'clock each Friday morning thinking a burglar was bursting through the bedroom window, only to recognise Sim's head coming through the curtains. 'Sshhh!' he'd go, struggling to find his lips with his finger and nearly putting out his eye instead.

I knew Sim and I were growing apart when he began to fart longer and louder than before. He had his own money now, so his improved prowess in this field may have been due to a different diet (beer and burgers). Whatever, I could no longer compete. He was now in Dad's league. On Saturdays, Sim would now hurry home after the game, so he could get ready to go out. I'd be watching the replay as he rushed away, awash in his Brut splash-on aftershave.

Suddenly, Sim was smitten. Lisa says she knew he'd be her husband the second she set eyes on him.

The Streaker

The first nude lady I actually saw in the flesh, so to speak, was stripper turned streaker Helen Demenico, who strutted her stuff at the first grand final I ever attended. It was 1982, Carlton versus Richmond. I cried as Slim Dusty sang the national anthem. I laughed when I saw the nude lady. I don't know why in either instance.

Midway through the third quarter, Carlton's ninth goal put them a point in front, and as the two teams waited for the ball to be brought back to the centre for the bounce, the crowd erupted. Wondering what was up, I followed the sea of pointing fingers and found my eyes falling to rest on what I would have assumed to be an apparition, had everyone else not seen the same thing. A football game and a naked female — I couldn't connect the two concepts. Beyond the breasts, it was her dark triangle of pubic hair that had me mesmerised. It seemed strange that I should be allowed to look. Seeing the same sight in any other circumstance would have constituted misbehaviour. It felt naughty but nice. Everybody was excited — except Wayne Johnston, Carlton vice-captain. Someone had to make a move, but I know blokes who questioned his methods when he shoved her out of the centre square. Well, with all the options, Johnno grabbed hold of her scarf!

Standing Room

That first grand final had me hooked. Crystal clear in my mind is the sight of Carlton players swapping jumpers with their vanquished opponents, wearing them like scalps. Running a lap of honour, pursued by unfit photographers, as the theme song blasted out of the sound system. Passing the premiership cup among themselves, popping champagne corks. From that moment on, the game took on a whole new meaning for me.

Standing-room tickets cost eleven dollars. Either you arrived early or it was a waste of time. An hour-long wait at the bar meant blokes took as many cans as they could carry back to their vantage point. Rather than putting their hard-won position in jeopardy by taking a toilet trip, most then preferred to piss into one of the cans they'd just emptied. Drinking steadily through the afternoon, they'd pick up successive tinnies from the selection around their feet, testing the temperature with their fingertips until they came across a coldie. As the afternoon wore on, the cans warmed up and such precautions were often neglected, resulting in the occasional eruption of spluttering and swearing. Simon and I displayed a smidgen of sophistication. Still on the soft drink, we used a four-litre Easy-Goer as our personal place to pee.

CHAPTER FOURTEEN

The Car Chase

Elliot looked a lot like Elvis Presley, early Vegas version. Able to take big grabs with one bite, he played full forward for Nottinghill Bs and kicked like David Cloke, then Richmond centre half-forward: both arms held out straight, holding the ball at its upper end, leaning back as it dropped onto the boot. It was the same style later adopted by Sydney's Warwick Capper. We could all impersonate David Cloke. Elliot didn't have to.

His bedroom smelt of mouse shit. He had a dozen of the dirty blighters, all fighting for space to run around on the minuscule ferris-wheel thing. Elliot was strange in that he barracked for North Melbourne *and* Michael Roach. That's right. As I said it. Both featured on his dufflecoat. He had blue and white stuff sewn all over it, with a yellow number eight ironed on the back, as worn by the Tiger spearhead.

Two or three years earlier, we went to Waverley Park to watch North Melbourne play Richmond. Elliot was in heaven. After the game, as we ran on the ground to kick the Sherrin, the one I'd won from *Inside Football*, I emphasised to him the importance of watching my prize wherever it went. Although the sky was littered with flying balls, the distinct yellow glow of my new footy was rare in the air and easy to trace. The night-game Sherrin was hard to come by and was an obvious target for thieves. It had been missing only a moment when I saw two blokes sprinting up the aisle steps between the seats, carrying my most treasured possession. I yelled out to Elliot and took off after them. They were a long way in front, but I was moving faster than I ever had before. Although they were twice my size and must've been eighteen, I was too furious to be frightened. I saw them go down the steel staircase at the back of the grandstand, opposite the main scoreboard, but by the time I got to ground level, they were half a mile away, running through the half-deserted carpark towards the man-made lake near the fenced-off freeway. Struggling to see through tears, I gave up.

Suddenly, I had an idea! I was close to the police locker rooms, where Dad had taken me once before. Bursting in, I spluttered something about two big boys nicking my brand-new ball. A couple of cops pulled on their pants, and asked me for directions as we drove off in the divvy-van, siren sounding. The robbers were halfway over the freeway fence when they realised they'd been rumbled. Fortunately for me, they chucked the footy in our direction and fled. I returned triumphant to the waiting Elliot, who may still be wondering exactly how I managed to retrieve the ball.

Part of Dad's occasional Saturday shift at Waverley Park involved escorting the coaches to and from their box at the breaks, which gave him access to all areas. He often remarked upon the filthy language used during team pep talks, claiming there was no need for grown men to speak that way. Afterwards, though, when I was waiting for him to change into his civvies, the swearing I would hear coming from him and his workmates was just as shocking, especially considering who it was coming from. I thought cops were supposed to set an example.

When not working at Waverley, Dad joined Mum most matches in the members' stand, fully equipped with thermos and bulky blankets. Choosing which team to support at the beginning of each game, Mum would start an argument while Dad was out of his seat, then expect him to finish it when he returned.

Waverley gave me frozen feet. Most of the day out there involved stomping on the spot to restart the circulation. Half-time featured Mike Williamson's on-screen interviews, usually with the day's opposing captains, interviewed before the game began. Any appearance by Mike Williamson inspired instant cries of: 'I tipped this' and 'He's not an octopus', two of the many famous quotes from his call of the legendary 1966 grand final, alongside Ted Whitten and 'Butch' Gale. Supporters of all sides know critical segments of that game's commentary word for word. For us St Kilda supporters, the lines are like our own Lord's Prayer, for that was the day of our triumph. The day St Kilda reigned supreme, by a single point. And the losing team? Collingwood, just to cap it all off! The winning point was booted by Barry Breen, who went on to play three hundred games, a milestone he reached in 1982. A limited edition (only twenty thousand!) wax-based parchment-paper commemoration of the occasion was printed, a copy of which I treasure to this day. It represents my connection to that glorious afternoon, before I was born, when St Kilda won the flag.

The SCG

When South Melbourne first relocated to Sydney, it seemed that Barry Round was chaired off the ground almost every week, even if they'd lost. I wondered whether Round had the luxury written into his contract, as some players were reluctant about uprooting their lives and the League was desperate to ensure the stars of that side made the transition. The Swans had all games at their new home televised from the start. We didn't support them, but if there was a game on the telly, we'd watch it. It was part of the League's overall plan to maintain interest in the move, while softening the blow for South supporters.

I'd been to South's old home ground, the Lakeside Oval, only once before it was made redundant. It was in 1980, and I remember the day for a ten-goal loss inspired both by Graham Teasdale's dominance and by a fella named John Roberts, who soared skywards to take what became the mark of the year. How sad that I was never to return.

Barry Round's Roman brand of post-match behaviour riled me. I think it was the way he played as well. He was obviously able, as his Brownlow Medal testifies, but he had an awkward way of moving. He seemed to suffer from a lack of coordination that became annoying when he repeatedly beat St Kilda's stars in the air. Round was a case of substance over style. When Carlton's David Rhys-Jones went for a run down the ground, he appeared to be moving in slow motion. I failed to understand why our players couldn't catch him. In fact, he was very fast on his feet. Some athletes are able to create an optical illusion. In his own way, big Barry was the same.

Colin Marshall was a lifelong Swans supporter and probably the first child in Australia to have a skinhead, or bonehead as we referred to it at the time. 'Marsh' took offence at my continual anti-Barry Round remarks, especially when I delivered them on his doorstep. One day, I rang his bell and greeted him with: 'Barry Round is shit'. I knew it would stir him up, but I didn't expect a smack in the eye for my efforts! We wrestled on his front lawn for fifteen minutes, fighting furiously until Marsh's mum came out and dragged him inside, packing me off home. Marsh had got me one in the mouth as he moved away. The taste of my own blood triggered my temper. His old man was a plumber, so there were plenty of pipes lying about the place. I picked one up and began inviting my friend outside, shouting towards the shut front door, swishing the pipe around over my head like Luke Skywalker with a lightsabre. I'd lost the plot by this point, and it was only his dad's sudden presence on the porch which saw me settle down. I'd officially taken things too far. Two days later, Marsh and I were mates again as usual.

The VFA

Marsh and his brothers all played for Waverley in the VFA second division. Waverley wore red and black vertical stripes, their best player being Laurie Fowler, formerly of Richmond and Melbourne. My mate was the youngest and most talented Marshall. Older brother Russell became a regular member of the senior side for a few seasons, while Malcolm, the eldest, was the Trevor Chappell of the trio — a borderline battler who benefited from the family connection.

Mr Marshall, Max, was a bloody good bloke. He assisted at Waverley Football Club in every capacity, over many years, earning the odd engraved pewter beer mug in recognition. Mrs Marshall had her hands full coping with what, essentially, appeared to be four variations on the one man. All worked in the plumbing business, all were steadfast South Melbourne supporters and all, the old man excepted, favoured heavy metal music. The Marshall brothers were into Metallica ten years before *Enter Sandman* shot to the top. Not satisfied with overseas bands like Iron Maiden and Motorhead, the Marshalls also formed the entire audience at gigs by little-known local outfits with names like Dirty Rats and Axatak. Dressed in sleeveless denim with steel studs, I attempted to appreciate the lifestyle for a good six months myself, but in the end, my heart wasn't in it.

As a footballer, Marsh was so far ahead of anyone our age, it was hard to fathom. His skills were unmatched. In primary and secondary school sides, he orchestrated the most amazing manoeuvres you could wish to see. I felt privileged to play in the same side, offering token assistance such as a shepherd while he wove one of his many spells. He often outplayed eight or nine opponents on his own. After a stint with the Fitzroy Under 19s, he went on to play first division for Oakleigh in the VFA, before becoming a hired gun for country and interstate sides. A curly-headed, courageous, prolific possession-winning centreman, Marsh did very well for himself, but I wondered: if he couldn't make it in the ultimate arena, just how good did you have to be?

During the mid–1980s, Waverley Football Club was blessed with a fabulous full forward whose solid build ensured he shared with Rene Kink the nickname 'Hulk': Paul Angelis. In reality, he looked more like an out-of-shape Sly Stallone with a soft perm. I once watched him kick nineteen goals in a game. Outstanding individual tallies were not unusual in the second division. While he led the competition's goal-kicking list, the club still hovered around the ladder's middle rungs. Local fire departments sent a truck along to VFA games, to sound the siren at each quarter's end. I recall a tight game when the truck took off halfway through the final quarter. All hell broke loose as the umpire blew his whistle, believing the siren to have sounded. Everyone and their uncle were over the fence and on the ground, offering their version of events. 'There's ten minutes left, mate. They've fucked off to a fire!'

Yarraville was one of Waverley's traditional rivals. The two teams fought tough, close encounters, and Yarraville had the division's other star spearhead, Mark Fotheringham. He helped himself to double figures during most matches, resplendent in his red, white and blue strip with its flying eagle on the front. With the lower level of skill came a lower level of supporter. The leader of Yarraville's cheer squad was known among opposition crowds as Fat Dacks (not to be confused with Fats, whose nickname was intended to be endearing, as in 'Fats Domino'), for reasons that are obvious. With classic Coke-bottle glasses and an ample girth, Fat Dacks conducted fellow fans in full voice, fighting against the odds to fit 'Fotheringham' into a rhythmic, clap-along chant. VFA games took place on Sundays. Fat Dacks sublet himself to the Footscray cheer squad on Saturdays, making him the western suburbs' most visible footy worshipper.

The Mordi Grandmas were a die-hard drove of blue-rinsed elderly women who went to all Mordialloc's matches, come hell or high water. Taking the moral high ground, the Mordi Grandmas had a keen ear for expletives, and were forever demanding apologies from those heard cussing in the crowd. Curious to know which words they considered unacceptable, we took turns one day at deliberately letting fly with feeble abuse. The weakest insult to cause offence was to be the winner.

'Get off the ground you bloody dole bludger', Simon yelled at one of the old ladies' idols. 'Ay, ay, ay. You mind what you're saying, son', one of them replied, taking the bait. 'It's hooligans like you who ruin it for the rest of us.' We all cheered Sim's success, slapped him on the back, and awarded him bonus points for eliciting the vintage term 'hooligan'. I imagine the old lady also considered boxing his ears.

A mate of ours once brought his own whistle to a game and created havoc by blowing it at various stages. Players stopped in their tracks, mistakenly believing the umpire had found a free kick. It was hilarious, until a hefty half-back jumped the fence and threatened to do random damage if it happened again.

During a VFA second division reserves grand final, I saw a player hit the umpire, then remove his jumper, presumably to prevent having his number taken. Hurdling the fence, he barged bare-chested through the crowd and disappeared into the street. The VFA was footy at its grassroots. A place for personalities to prosper. It also gave us something to do on a Sunday now the Nottinghill B team had disbanded, laid to rest following one too many dire defeats.

CHAPTER FIFTEEN

The Dreams

I often arise from distinct, detailed enjoyable dreams feeling disappointed as I realise its events were only imagined. No matter how hard I try to slip back into slumber, I can never recapture the same situation.

At fifteen, I seduced both Laura Summers and Judy Bloomsbury in one go. Together. I don't know why but we were in the back room of a pinball parlour. The two most-wanted women at Syndal Tech! They'd never noticed me before but there we were, the three of us, having sizzling sex as someone played Space Invaders outside. I woke up with my loins in a lather.

Though I wished that dream was reality, I'd swap it for the time I was ten. Riding my scooter to the local shops, I saw a news-stand, upon which *The Herald* headline screamed 'SAINTS SIGN SIX MILLION DOLLAR MAN'.

As I read of how he was going to be our new full forward, I suddenly sat up awake to the stone cold truth. Instead of a sci-fi star with his own TV show, the real papers that morning said St Kilda had signed a half-back-flanker from Footscray, named Albert Smedts. Which didn't quite have the same ring to it.

I can't say whether it was a guess or based on actual evidence but shortly after my dirty dreams began, Dad called me into his room, 'their' room, and showed me two hundred bucks and a box of condoms in the bedside drawer.

'These are for you but only if you need 'em,' he said in a swift, simple statement which amounted to my 'lesson about life'. No birds. No bees. No bullshit.

Australia was not held in high esteem by the international showbiz set during the 1970s. Major musical acts rarely included us in their tours and movie stars on promotional circuits hardly ever set foot on our shores. When Oscar Goldman announced he'd be arriving on a whirlwind publicity trip, it was almost as exciting as being given the Six Million Dollar Man doll as a Christmas gift. The doll ranks alongside my first football as the most perfect present I ever received. We would have preferred Steve Austin himself to visit, but if we had to settle for the doctor who built his bionic bits, then so be it. And anyway, Oscar wasn't exactly an unknown. After all, he had his own action figure. (True! It came with a briefcase, containing confidential documents, that exploded if opened the wrong way. The right way was explained in a secret set of instructions.)

Simon and I talked Dad into driving us all the way out to the airport, in the hope we might spot Oscar coming out of Customs. We were surprised Dad let us take the day off school. Maybe he wanted a look himself. Although excited, we were also a bit embarrassed about the whole affair, so we kept it quiet from our friends. In the car we sat silently, autograph books in hand. Five miles from Tullamarine airport, we hit an almighty traffic jam. It turned out every other kid in Melbourne had the same idea. Oscar got a bigger welcome than The Beatles.

The Dancing Queen

Mum and Dad often attended dinner dances, returning in the early hours 'three sheets to the wind'. At one such do, Mum had danced with Stewart Lord, footballing twin brother of the 1962 Brownlow medallist, Geelong's Alistair Lord. She claimed this was 'no big deal', though the frequency with which she repeated the story served to cast serious doubt on this disclaimer.

My parents felt it imperative for their sons' future social success that we also learn a step or two, and at age sixteen Mark and Simon were each forced to attend the nearby Swindon Dance Academy. Luckily, however, most of my parents' good intensions had been relaxed or forgotten by the time my turn came, so I avoided this monumental embarrassment. Not long afterwards, karma contrived to see me sucked in as partner to somebody's daughter at her debut.

I'd originally declined the request to partner her at her debut — debutante balls were not big on my wish list, and I doubt Trevor Barker ever bothered with such things — but the girl's associates conducted a campaign to change my mind. I was flattered, and tried to explain that it was the fancy footwork I was wary of, not their friend. Given my history with females generally, I was in no position to refuse any advances, and perhaps that's why, eventually, I accepted. In addition to white gloves and a poorly fitting tuxedo, I was expected to don a cummerbund for the occasion. A cummerbund! Is this the ugliest, most unnecessary item of clothing in existence? Even the word is unsightly. I mean, look at it: cummerbund. The cummerbund's purpose, apart from holding in an unsightly beer-gut on a groom's big day, remains a riddle to me.

Weeks of practice preceded the event. Despite all this, my attempts to trip the light fantastic were abysmal and, for her, undoubtedly painful. Among the other male partners, the only one seen to move with grace was a bloke named Andrew Phillips, who went on to display similar finesse as a rover for Carlton, with the occasional spell in a forward pocket. Isn't it always the way? He could dance without looking stupid *and* he could play footy.

You may have guessed that there was no romance for me in the aftermath of this debacle. At the after-party, I was too busy dealing with the fact that people had just seen me 'dance' in a public place to even attempt a pash. I was rooted, but not in the right way. It's all very well for her, I thought. No-one seemed to care that I still had not made *my* debut.

The Friendship

Sim's mate from Monash High, Graeme Peddle, had a younger brother who went to Syndal Tech, Brenton. Sim asked one day if I knew of him. I didn't, but decided to arrange a meeting. It was the beginning of a beautiful friendship, as they say in the classics. Australia had just won the America's Cup, Prime Minister Bob Hawke announcing on TV that, 'Any boss who sacks someone for taking today off is a bum', and the mood was ripe for running amok.

Brenton Peddle and I shared the same interests and fast gained a local reputation as risk-takers. We were the only people our age who didn't care about parental curfews. We didn't fight the idea. It was fine by us. While our mates were out on secretive beach-side weekends or sneaking scotch into blue-light discos, Peddle and I enjoyed ourselves by watching videos, eating pizza and playing pool in the extension his dad had built on the back of their house. Peddle was popular for a number of reasons, among them his precise impersonation of Rick from *The Young Ones*. Otherwise, he was envied and admired for possessing the ability to vomit on demand. Most of us could make ourselves burp, but Peddle's was a trick to treasure.

Hard as nails and totally fearless on the footy field, a trait he shared with his then look-a-like Dermot Brereton, Peddle was not particularly impressed by attention from the Tigers. Having been spotted by a Richmond talent scout when playing for Oakleigh Districts, he was invited down for a run during the pre-season. On arrival, Peddle realised that he was one of fifty or sixty fellas in the same boat. Mathematically assessing his actual chances and calculating the commitment required to become the cream, he decided it wasn't worth staying for the traditional final four laps — it was roast-dinner night, and if he hurried, he'd just make it home in time.

When we turned eighteen and the curfew was lifted, Peddle and I embarked on a journey of discovery. We had some catching up to do. We began what the others had become bored with: alcohol and uproar.

The Cricket

September aside, the days following Christmas were among any year's best. The Boxing Day Test match demanded an early start if we wanted a decent seat. The whole family went every year, without fail. Well, almost the whole family. Nana stayed home and slept. 'Come on Aussie, come on, come on', sang Simon and I on the train to the MCG. 'Lillee's pounding down like a machine . . . '

Mark, Simon and I sat in Bay Thirteen, while Mum and Dad took a seat in the stands. I couldn't whistle, which made me the odd one out whenever a bikini-clad beauty wandered up the aisle. I could laugh, though, so I wasn't left out during the occasional collie-dog frisbee-catching demonstrations, one of many activities on offer throughout the day. During a match against the West Indies, a Caribbean band went around the ground on the back of a truck during the lunch break, only to be pelted with hot dogs, ice cubes, empty cans, oranges — anything and everything. The sky was literally raining rubbish.

Luckily, the lead singer took it with good grace, taunting crowd members for their lack of accuracy.

I was also a keen cricket fan. I was delighted when John Dyson jumped like a soccer goalkeeper to take that classic catch. I'd stayed awake all night under the bedclothes hearing debutante Dirk Welham make a hundred in England on my tranny. I'd even met Jeff Moss, the Victorian captain. Fats was his next-door neighbour. I chose to join a team purely to fill in my Saturday afternoons when the footy season finished, but struggled to find a team who believed in me. I'd only played with a tennis ball, one side covered in sticky tape to encourage swing. I wouldn't know my abilities with a cricket ball until somebody gave me a go.

Following numerous net sessions among the lower levels of Mount Waverley and Ashwood cricket clubs, I'd achieved nothing more than fielding at fine leg. In this position for Ashwood one afternoon, I was rudely awoken from a daydream by the sudden arrival of the ball, an easy, unseen catching opportunity. It bounced off my shoulder, knocking me to the ground and the ball into the fence for four. The incident did little to enhance my reputation.

Oakleigh Districts, my next cricket club, proved to be third time lucky. Brenton Peddle invited me down for a game. Due to a buck's turn the previous evening, the coach was nowhere to be seen, so Peddle's dad, Bluey, took over the reins. Bluey Peddle was the Keith Miller, the Max Walker, the Simon O'Donnell of Oakleigh Districts. Excelling as a footballer *and* cricketer for the club in the

1960s, his name was engraved in gold leaf on every wall. He and his wife, Betty, were local legends. An acute victim of ozone-layer depletion, Bluey wore Greg Chappell-style hats before Greg Chappell did. He knew I wanted to be a fast bowler, and within half an hour, I was marking out my run-up for the first time in a proper match. Two balls later I was on a hat trick. It didn't eventuate, but I ended the over with a double-wicket maiden. Moving into Third Grade, I enjoyed several glorious summers squeezed in the back of the captain's ute with the rest of the team, making our way to matches and singing along with the songs on the radio.

Ours was the sort of competition where bowlers often had their approach to the wicket interrupted by slips fieldsmen suddenly chundering from the after-effects of a heavy Friday night. In reality, I was as crap at cricket as I was at footy, but it was a relaxing atmosphere. Training was a place to perfect my cricketing impressions. Bowling like Bob Willis cheered everyone up. He moved his neck like a chicken when he ran. Gladstone Small was easy. He had no neck at all. We competed to see who could do which players best.

One day, left to my own devices, I was hitting a ball against a wall in our back yard. It was summer, cricket season. We had a makeshift pitch down the side of the house, and played almost every afternoon, though on this day, all the kids I knew were away. Mum was putting the washing on the line when, out of the blue, she offered to roll the arm over. I went along with the idea and found it fun, taking it easy on Mum's surprisingly accurate off-breaks. Suddenly, she served up a full toss so tantalising, I couldn't help but hit it with all my might. Mum's dormant reflexes snapped into action. Like a lizard plucking a fly from mid-air, she stuck out her right hand and held an amazing catch. It was sensational by any standard. She just stood there, looking shocked, surprised and particularly pleased with herself. For a split second, I felt humiliated. Caught and bowled by my Mum! Then I realised what a unique event I had witnessed, and relaxed enough to enjoy her enthusiasm. 'What a bottler!' she cried. It was a magical moment and I felt even closer to Mum than I had beforehand.

Retrieving cricket balls from up on our roof was relaxing if I was by myself. Treading cautiously across the tiles, with no-one waiting below for the ball's return in order to begin a game again, I could sit up there for as long as I wanted, watching the world go by. It was peaceful, away from everybody and provided an excellent view of the neighbourhood.

CHAPTER SIXTEEN

The Fehring Flyer

In the search for a ruckman to replace the long-serving Jeff Sarau, St Kilda signed Geelong's Jeff Fehring. Solid and serviceable, if not highly skilled, Fehring couldn't crack it with the Cats. There, he'd faced the same dilemma as did Stephen Taubert at Essendon — too much tall timber. Just as the Madden brothers prevented Taubert from establishing himself at Essendon, Fehring had to move over for the bigger and better Rod Blake and John Mossop at Geelong. Unlike Taubert, however, who flowered and became a force when he moved to the Sydney Swans, Fehring remained a second-string selection with his new club, the Saints, yet he nevertheless found fame with a kick that became part of footy folklore.

Moorabbin was packed for St Kilda's match against Collingwood. With his wispy, rust-coloured hair and the beginnings of a double-chin, Fehring was making mincemeat out of reigning Brownlow medallist Peter Moore in their ruck duels around the ground. He was having an official 'purple patch'. Suddenly, a scuffle saw his name and number entered into the umpire's notebook. Fehring was not happy. Moments later, still furious, he accepted a free kick at the bounce. From behind the centre circle, he launched into what was obviously a prodigious punt. An intended torpedo, it had already travelled a decent distance when an air current appeared to catch the ball and carry it even further. He'd kicked it as straight as it was long, and as the ball bounced in the goal square and through the big sticks, the crowd's reaction was chaotic. Using film footage for verification, the kick was measured during the week at 93 metres — an awesome achievement. And while this anecdote may seem mundane and unworthy of inclusion in the memoirs of the supporter of any other team, what with fitting in all the tales of premiership glory, we at Moorabbin had to be thankful for small mercies. If that meant making a big deal out of the biggest kick, we weren't too proud to do so.

The Recruits

When recruiting from other clubs, St Kilda aimed for the novelty players. I'd like to think it was a coincidence, but when it came to coughing up the cash, it was the players with a cult following or some sort of negative notoriety that found their way to Moorabbin, creating a myth that St Kilda was a den for discards. Prince of this parade was Mark Jackson. Jacko began his footy career by kicking the ton for the Richmond reserves, but was unable to gain senior selection ahead of Michael Roach and Brian Taylor, so defected to the Demons. He became an immediate sensation in Melbourne's senior side, where his inimitable style and high scoring made him a legend. So did playing with his false teeth removed.

Jacko's greatest coup was to capitalise on his high media profile by unleashing the novelty single *I'm an Individual*, the first bona fide hit by a footballer. Not content with his reputation as a recording artist, Jacko then embarked on a major marketing campaign as the Energizer battery bloke, a job which saw his head plastered on billboards right across America and made him a lot of money. Already a star on the sportman's night circuit, he released his autobiography, then won a role on *The Highwayman*, a second-rate US sci-fi series in which he played some sort of futuristic crime-fighter. True, he may now be reduced to appearing in Jenny Craig commercials, but Mark Jackson made more out of the public's fascination for all things football than any who came before him.

Silvio Foschini arrived at Moorabbin in a blaze of controversy, having refusing to relocate to Sydney when South Melbourne became the Sydney Swans. He'd exploded onto the scene two seasons earlier as a squinty-eyed roving forward-pocket capable of kicking spectacular goals. Channel Seven's Sandy Roberts delighted in crying: 'Hi ho Silvio!' as the tiny Italian cartwheeled through the pack to score another six points from what appeared to be a handstand position. Foschini won a restraint-of-trade case against his former club, blowing the League's swap market wide open. Paul

Morwood and his combed beard followed, subsequently winning a Best and Fairest with the Saints. For a few days after Silvio's successful court case, it appeared any player could join any club whenever he wanted. The League managed to close the loophole, but not before St Kilda had gained two instant stars.

Other St Kilda recruits from other clubs included Geelong wingman Robert 'Scratcher' Neal. Whenever I saw Scratcher, I heard *Duelling Banjos* from *Deliverance*, yet Simon and I once saw him, after a game, with a covergirl on each arm. René Kink arrived via Essendon, overweight and two years past his use-by-date. He played a couple of good games for us, but was generally more 'Bulk' than 'Hulk' by the time he arrived. Jimmy Krakouer came from the Kangaroos and played a few great games. During one match at the MCG, he clouted Collingwood's Shane Kerrison fair in the face, having taken offence at his tagging techniques, and we certainly couldn't complain at that.

Brian Wilson, whom we had hated with a passion when he was a Melbourne man, became a cult figure on account of his outrageous arrogance. Every goal, he celebrated like a last-second flag-winner. He'd run around the ground as if doing a lap of honour, giving high-fives to supporters strung along the fence, which looked ridiculous if we were ten goals down late in a game and it was the first kick he'd had all day.

Enrico Misso's career highlight had been a seat on the Bombers' reserves bench until the Saints managed to fit him into the firsts. It was my view he should have been nicknamed 'Givima', especially by the selectors. Rohan Smith, the bald albino-looking bloke from Port Adelaide, was at least a laugh, providing supporters with the only excuse they're ever likely to have to wear rubber 'bald wigs' in public and in the daytime. We badly needed such diversions from the on-field action.

Simon O'Donnell rolled up with an enviable reputation, having kicked a billion goals as a schoolboy superstar with Assumption College, the most successful breeding ground the VFL had ever known. Unfortunately for us, his football career fell by the wayside as his cricket career prospered. I met O'Donnell through a mutual mate a few years after he'd finished playing footy. He recoiled as I reminded him of his first game, where he was decked behind play by Michael Tuck, of all people. (Tuck, though a fine footballer, was not renowned for the rough stuff.)

I also recounted the origin of O'Donnell's nickname: 'Scuba'. This he'd earned by taking a 'dive' after being belted at Arden Street by Phil Carman, then playing his first and only season for North Melbourne. Not surprisingly, I was at the game with my brother, and we, along with most people at the ground that day, feared for O'Donnell's immediate future when he went down. It happened moments before the final siren was due. The situation looked serious. The special stretcher came out, and they constructed it around him as Carman's number was noted. The crowd cheered their best wishes as he was carried off the field. Unbeknown to us, but etched in his team-mates' memories, he was apparently up and walking about within seconds of the stretcher entering the dressing rooms, fit as a fiddle.

Then came what I called the reprieve recruits. If a player had so much as a sniff of success about them, St Kilda's door was always open. From Hawthorn, we welcomed Andrew Bennett, Michael Moncrieff, Peter Russo and Sean Ralph-Smith. Even if they'd previously been regulars in the reserves, St Kilda's committee rolled out the red carpet. 'Hell, he at least trained with the proper players. He must have *something* that might rub off on us.' Correct. What they had was a skill level no longer sufficient to remain in the firsts at their former clubs. From Carlton came 'Wow' Jones, Ken Sheldon, Alex Marcou and Ian Aitken. Many gave the Saints great service, but only after their original clubs had found somebody faster and fitter.

In 1980, we actually signed a bloke called Mick Jez. He had no positive history as a player whatsoever, and to this day, I *honestly* believe he was signed because his name sounded like 'Jezza' and he also came from Carlton. Another recruit's claim to fame was that he'd won some novelty contest in which he was the fastest to run up a steep hill with a sack of spuds on his shoulders, dragging a tractor tyre behind him. It concerned me to think that while other clubs' scouts were scouring suburban and country competitions for new talent, ours were watching *It's a Knockout*.

The greatest shemozzle a St Kilda recruit created was what the media termed 'The Doug Cox Affair'. St Kilda signed Cox from Woodville, South Australia, in 1981. On fine form immediately, it was revealed midway through the season that he had initially agreed to terms with the Tigers before arriving at Moorabbin. Richmond ignored the oversight until they saw him in action, then suddenly chose to point out the illegalities in his playing permit. An investigation saw St Kilda forfeit its premiership points in punishment. We'd won only two games to that stage of the season, so the loss was neither large nor significant, but at twelve years of age, I found it absolutely shattering. Watching details of the crisis on the TV news, I gravely announced to Mum: 'It's gonna be a long day', exhaling heavily, in a brave attempt to brace us all for the fear and furore we faced in the immediate future. I then set off to purchase the papers, perversely excited about the boost such a huge story would give my scrapbook.

Doug Cox survived all the animosity, only to get snotted, good and proper, in his first game back by Richmond's Kevin Bartlett. It had been a game of high tension, as it had been the protest by the Tigers that had set events in motion in the first place and had robbed us of our only two wins. And of all people to be belted by, Kevin Bartlett was particularly embarrassing. A short, skinny rover with five hairs combed across his head. How would I ever face school on Monday?

The Music

Some time around 1980, *Footy Favourites* was unleashed on an unsuspecting public. An album consisting of songs selected and sung by the stars themselves, it represented, without doubt, the darkest day in recording history. Each team's representative was chosen for his football skills, not for any vocal ability. Trevor Barker crooned *I Can See Clearly Now*, while Footscray full forward Kelvin Templeton made a bid for worst song on the album with his rendition of *Who's Sorry Now?*. (We all were, from first note to last.) However, it was Collingwood captain Ray Shaw who provided the nadir: the most dismal, disastrous version of *Danny Boy* delivered anywhere, by anybody, under any circumstances. It was so harrowing as to be beyond humour. He deserved to have been disciplined for such a disgrace.

The funniest performance came from exceptionally skinny Melbourne champion Robbie Flower, who decided to go with *Macho Man*. Flower managed a sports store at Forest Hill Shopping Centre in nearby Nunawading, and we'd regularly remind him of his musical moment from a safe spot around the corner: 'I want to be a macho, macho man'.

Some time down the track, with the horror of *Footy Favourites* beginning to fade, flashy Sydney Swans full forward Warwick Capper, perhaps swept away by the grand ambitions of newly arrived entrepreneur owner Dr Geoffrey Edelston, released a single, *I Only Take What's Mine*. The less said about this effort, the better. There are few better warnings of the dangers of straying outside your area of expertise (which at the time, for Warwick, was standing on opponents' heads and hauling in spectacular high marks). With his talent for taking spekkies and his habit of mating with models, Capper caught my imagination much as Trevor Barker had done years earlier. Though remaining steadfastly loyal to my main man, I did take a newspaper picture into the hairdresser's and demanded a Capper cut. I came out looking like Tina Turner.

The Troubles

For no logical reason, except perhaps for the fact that I had become a pubescent prick overnight, I began to give Mum a hard time. It became so bad that at one point, Dad took me to the cop station for a heart-to-heart with one of his colleagues in the hope I'd settle down before he had to strangle me. School fared worse for my suddenly swinging moods. With real life beginning to take on a heavy vibe, my other existence, as a Saints supporter, took on extra importance and the ritual of going to a game was even more relaxing.

Four 'n' Twenty pies were a staple part of Saturday's diet. Mum's bread rolls 'filled a hole', but there was nothing to beat a hot meat pie at half-time. 'Hot pies, cold drinks!', were offered around the ground, but we all knew the opposite applied. One buyer, having been assured by the acne-ridden pie-boy that the pies were indeed hot, was far from thrilled to discover just how false advertising can be. 'It's stone fucking cold!', he yelled after the pie-boy, now fifteen feet further down the aisle, and threw the pie perfectly, splattering it all over the offender's neck.

Simon once managed a similar manoeuvre at the MCG. South Melbourne's demise saw Fats slowly become a Saints supporter, and before long he was a permanent, passionate member of our long-standing Moorabbin line-up. He was with us the day that Simon bit into a ham and cheese roll. Simon was sick of ham in his rolls and claimed to have specifically asked Mum to give it a miss. He fished out the offending ham slice and flung it skyward in frustration. We watched as the scrunched-up ham unfolded itself and flew flat through the air, spinning in circles like a frisbee before flopping neatly onto a balding bloke's head, the margarine acting as an adhesive. As he looked around for the enemy, I'm surprised that the sight of us three collapsed in fits of uncontrollable laughter didn't give the game away. Fats was so far gone for so long afterwards, we feared he might have a heart attack. Even now, all we have to say is: 'Ham on head', and he's off.

CHAPTER SEVENTEEN

The Terrorist

Each year I was on the periphery of Syndal Tech's first football team, occasionally getting a run in the back pocket so that one of the proper players could have a rest. My inclusion in the squad each year was a direct result of my mate, Marsh, feeding me the ball during the preliminary games. I wasn't very good, but it took a while for me to work it out. I did play, however, for long enough to enjoy the classic personality quirk of a kid we called Big Ted. An able, workmanlike ruckman shot to star status by virtue of his sheer size for such a young age, Big Ted was a pacifist who could withstand any kind of physical challenge and all manner of verbal abuse *unless* it referred to his family. No matter how hackneyed the remark, Big Ted flew off the handle every time.

'My grandma does not wear army boots mate!', he'd be screaming as the rest of us attempted to pry him off the poor bastard he was pummelling.

By fifth form, I well knew my limitations, settling for what we called Yobbo Footy, a standard at which I finally excelled. This was essentially everyone who couldn't get a game in the firsts, plus a few others who loped around for a laugh, playing against each other in a mad, bad free-for-all. The older HSC students joined in, and it often got out of hand. I still have a perfectly circular scar on the back of my skull from somebody's football-boot stud as evidence of the 'endeavour' involved. The games were school-sanctioned (under another name, of course — 'Fitness Football' or something) and were umpired by our Physical Education teachers. We had two of them. Mr Lang, a stocky, muscular Chinaman who had represented his home country as a weightlifter in Olympic competition, and Mr Preece.

Mr Preece was Australian, yet he was an American college movie cliché: a tight white T-shirt, whistle dangling around his neck, humiliate-the-fat-kid-in-front-of-his-friends type of bloke. From time to time whilst umpiring the Yobbo games, he liked to hand his whistle over to Mr Lang and join in, quickly becoming over-enthusiastic and making Micky Conlan-style runs down the ground, steamrolling a couple of skinny kids on the way.

It would be an understatement to say Mr Preece was unpopular. A single drop of rain saw him call us all inside immediately, saying he didn't want anyone catching cold during his class, but we all knew the real reason: vanity. His thinning blond crop was 'pfoofed up' with a hairdryer and mountains of mousse, creating a sort of human-hair fairy-floss. Torrential rain would have unravelled the bald truth, and that was *not* an option.

One afternoon, before another Yobbo match, the students decided that Mr Preece was going down. The plan was agreed; the hatchet man was not. With numerous nominations on the table, it was decided to simply wait for the right situation to arise. Early in the first quarter, the moment came and Mr Preece fled the field, shouting, swearing and cupping a bleeding nose in his hands. And who was the hero among us young men? To everyone's surprise, it was Conman, a strong, silent, Charles Bronson type. Conman and I had been mates at school for a couple of years before I managed to score an invitation around to his house. There, I was amazed to discover shelves full of footy trophies won with his local club. The weird thing was, the rest of his shelves were full of books on philosophy.

Conman had never attempted to get a game in the school side, though he would certainly have succeeded. I, on the other hand, busted a gut to be included, despite the certainty that I'd fail. His strange and inaccurate kicking style defied his possession-winning ability and prevented most of us from realising how good he actually was. Conman chose not to try for the school side because, he said, somewhat enigmatically, 'I don't agree with the idealism behind the selection process'.

Whatever, he'd hit our nemesis full in the face under the guise of trying to punch the ball away from behind. It was the perfect crime, committed under the very nose of authority. Aside from a kick awarded against him by a slightly smirking Mr Lang, Conman escaped further punishment. Having washed off the blood, Mr Preece saw no option but to end the game, claiming it was about to rain.

Too humiliated to play among us again, Mr Preece nevertheless found other ways of expressing his aggression. He had the charming and stylish habit of standing with his hands down the front of his tracksuit pants, thumbs hooked over the waistband. One morning at main assembly, he caught me and a couple of mates making fun of this stance. Furious, he marched us down to the gym and ordered us to wait outside the weights room, a concrete chamber with a window facing a brick wall. Moments later, he returned with a student teacher. They were going to talk to us individually, he said, to find out 'exactly what we found so funny'.

Mr Preece had decided to slap us around the weights room. His 'witness' would no doubt insist that any complaint we made was nonsense. The first of us was in there for ten minutes before reappearing in tears. By the time the second student stepped out, equally shaken, I'd devised my plan. Upon entering the room, I announced that I knew what was going on and there was no way they'd get away with it. This put them off their stride long enough for me to issue my ultimatum. 'Touch me and I'll tell. It's as simple as that.' Not the sort of thing you'd ever hear Chuck Norris holler, but I was desperately trying to bluff my way out of a belting. Somehow, I survived.

Dad was singularly unimpressed when I told him about Mr Preece's methods. Infuriated, he stormed off to see the school principal next morning, demanding an assurance that such an incident would never happen again. That evening at the kitchen table, I was told to stop shit-stirring and to steer clear of trouble. As far as dad was concerned, the matter was over. Until the following day, that is.

Mr Preece must have taken the principal's reprimand to heart, because he approached me in the yard at lunchtime and presented me with some paperwork. 'This', he said, 'is a letter from my solicitor. It says that I will not be intimidated by anybody at my place of employment, especially your father. If I don't hear from him within two days, retracting everything said so far, I'll have him up in court.' Obviously, unaware of my old man's occupation, Mr Preece was way out of his depth.

I had never seen Dad look so angry. Once again, he met with the principal and asked to see Mr Preece, but this time, he eventually demanded that the two of them be left alone in the office. Mr Preece avoided me from that day. No law suits surfaced. I'm not sure exactly what happened, but I doubt Dad said sorry.

Not all the staff at Syndal Tech rubbed me up the wrong way. My drama teacher was actress Maggie Doyle, who had appeared in the film of David Williamson's fabulous play about football, *The Club*. Artistic types may say it's actually about the politics and power prevalent within a corporate organisation, but to us it was about football, and here at Syndal Tech was one of its stars. Admittedly, she was on screen for only a few seconds, as the new recruit's girlfriend, but it qualified as fame as far as we were concerned.

Staff Versus Students

A curious concept at Syndal Tech was the annual staff versus students footy match. The whole school was given the afternoon off to attend. In front of such a large audience, the game provided an ideal opportunity to impress girls you hoped to grope. The staff were rarely able to field a full side, so they invited former stars of the student team to return for a run-around. As these substitutes had to arrange a day off from plumbing pipes, fixing Fairlanes or whatever else their work involved, they were keen to make an impact. Being neither staff nor students, there was no responsibility in regard to the rough stuff, meaning players on our side suffered.

Somehow, I managed to make the students' team (a situation that in hindsight seems suspicious) and found myself at full forward. A dedicated dickhead, I played to the capacity crowd by wearing a wrap-around bandanna, like Axl Rose from Guns and Roses. I'd like to think it was for show, but I was probably serious.

Despite being predictably hammered by the fully grown former students making their care-free comebacks, I managed to kick five goals before half-time. One was on the run! I can see it now. Leading out from the goal square, I let 'em know what I wanted. 'On me tits!', I screamed at the approaching wingman. The ball came my way, but fell several metres short. Grabbing it on the first bounce, I swivelled on my left foot, booted with my right and bang! Straight through the middle. It was a highlight of my football career.

Andrew Barnett, our usual full forward, was crook, so played in the pocket. Andrew and his identical twin, Grant, were international water-skiing champions, with faces and physiques in the Grant Kenny mould. We watched them compete on the Yarra at Moomba each March. Both fine footballers, they had been quiet for most of the match. Midway through the final quarter, I'd kicked six and was on fire. The ball came forward again, and with confidence in my newfound form, I flew for what I sensed would be a screamer. There I was, perched on someone's shoulders, perfectly poised to take a huge grab. But as my mates and a gaggle of girls looked on, Andrew Barnett leapt even higher, from behind, and held what I later heard was the mark of the millennium. I didn't see it myself, because as the pack collapsed beneath him, I landed on top and cushioned the high-flyer's fall. In the process, his foot, followed by the rest of his body weight, came crashing down on my testicles. While Barnett bathed in glory, I was carried off in a semi-coma, trying desperately to count my cods. Like the *Challenger* space-shuttle that very same week, I had experienced a 'major malfunction'. A piercing pain pulsed throughout my whole package. I mused on why only cricketers wear protectors.

CHAPTER EIGHTEEN

Half-Mast

Former Saint Val Perovic (a huge Yugoslav who somehow prompted crowds to shout 'Woof!' whenever he booted the ball) felt my fury one afternoon about fifteen minutes after he'd knocked Trevor Barker unconscious in the last quarter of a home game against Carlton. Barker was stretchered off the ground following the clash, for which Perovic was reported. As the siren sounded to end the match, I ran onto the field and fought my way through the throng. Spotting Perovic through tear-filled eyes, making his way off the field, I took aim with my flagpole. Then, on the run, I cracked him in the shins as hard as I could before disappearing through the crowd. I heard him swear, so it must have hurt. 'Suffer in your jocks', I muttered to myself.

Nana had sewn my flag together after I'd saved up for the material. I'd attempted an earlier version of my own, using white cotton and fabric dye, but the end result was a disaster. There's a skill to waving a flag, especially in a strong wind. To avoid it tangling up on itself, a flag needs to be waved in the style my Mum taught me to stir gravy

— like drawing a figure eight. The bigger the flag, or the thicker the gravy, the more strength is required. I carried my flag to matches as a soldier does his bayonet into battle. Although her eyesight was fading, Nana's flag stood sturdy, a fine example of her sewing-machine mastery.

Nana remained fit and healthy until, aged ninety, she had a 'funny turn'. The hospital, unable to find anything specific the matter with her, sent her home to rest. That night when I tiptoed into her darkened room to say good night, Nana told me the funny turn had given her a fright but that when she'd lost consciousness, she'd seen a beautiful bright light coming towards her. I told her she'd feel better after a good sleep, then kissed her on the cheek and went to watch a bit of telly before bed. She had a delicate smell to her, like talcum powder. She died that night.

CHAPTER NINETEEN

The Cheeky Boy

Each week, true football supporters stick to their own pre-game regimen as strictly as do the players they go to see. Saturday mornings in our house were a hive of activity. During the early days, we'd wake up and watch Daryl and Ossie. When *Hey Hey It's Saturday* moved to an evening timeslot, we'd watch music videos, then listen to the Coodabeen Champions. In either era, we'd follow this by slipping into our Saints jumpers and having a kick outside.

Meanwhile, Mum lovingly made the rolls. Each week, without fail, Simon and I received two bread rolls each, plastic-wrapped and paper-bagged. We found most games too entrancing to consider queuing up for food. Besides, there's not much worse than hearing a huge roar from the crowd when you're waiting in a line, away from the action, getting anxious about what's going on. Around midday, our mates would arrive: Shane from Syndal Tech, plus supporters of other sides, these latter being a constantly changing cast, depending on who the Saints played that day.

One morning, as Simon and I engaged in boisterous, brotherly behaviour with a footy on the front lawn, a boy we didn't know walked down our driveway. He wore a St Kilda jumper and looked to be about twelve. Politely, he announced his intentions, speaking slowly, as if he'd learned the lines: 'Excuse me. My name's Jason and I live around the corner. I've seen you two on Saturday mornings going off to the game. Would you mind if I came along each week, 'cos my Mum won't let me go by myself?'. His initiative was endearing. Jason had a Ginger Meggs face framed by a four-corner fringe, and was as meek as a mouse for the first two seasons. When kicking the footy after the final siren, we'd remind ourselves to give Jason a regular go, as he was half our height and a timid type. Unable to kick the designated distance, he'd run half the way before putting boot to ball.

Eventually he became hardened, but only after his heart was broken. One day, following a fantastic last-minute win at Moorabbin, Jason joined thousands of other supporters on the field, running towards the players' race, St Kilda flag held high. As the players pushed their way through the delirium and down into the dressing rooms, the wind flapped Jason's flag straight into Tony Lockett's face. Not known at that point for his public-relations prowess, and understandably annoyed, Plugger snatched the flag and tore it in half with his bare hands. Jason could not be consoled. Nor could he see the funny side. 'The fat bastard', he sniffled tearfully as we headed back towards the car.

Lockett's bestial reaction to the flagpole affair was an eye-opener for Young Jason. While not yet a fully fledged cynic, he was no longer the naïve young lad we had known to that point. Although the bad feelings were fleeting, hating his hero had hit him hard. It was the wake-up call we all receive at some stage. Someone, somewhere, lets you down without warning, and suddenly the easy ride is over. Jason's mental maturity caught up with his physical development, and in the space of two weeks, he metamorphosed from a mouse into a monster. The little shit started sitting on our shoulders during kick-to-kick. It hurt. It was humiliating. I felt a similar sting the day somebody younger than me played in St Kilda's senior side. (It was Robert Harvey, if you *must* know.) Both events damaged my ego.

I Marked Barker's Goal

One miserable, muddy afternoon at Moorabbin, a remarkable event took place during an otherwise unremarkable match. I marked a goal booted by Trevor Barker. This was, without doubt, the only moment in my life, to this point, that really mattered. Like the scene in the Twisties commercial, where the action man in the movie steps off the screen and into the cinema audience to get the girl he's sighted, fiction became fact as my fingers gripped the football. Trevor Barker had kicked the ball to me during a real match! Obviously, that was not his actual intention, but as his eyes followed the ball through the big sticks and into my eager arms, there was a millisecond when we were as one. Then he turned away, the centre of his team-mates' accolades, as I hugged the ball hard to my chest. Eventually, surrounding envious onlookers gave up trying to wrestle it away from me, thus allowing me the thrill of kicking an actual game ball back onto the ground.

I say it was an unremarkable match because I can't recall a thing about the rest of the game. The information-gathering component of my usually reliable memory for all things St Kilda was temporarily paralysed by the above-mentioned magical moment. Whether we won or lost is irrelevant (though I could have a bloody good guess). The fact that nobody else in the world (except, perhaps, my brother) is aware of the event's significance to me is also unimportant. In a full life, a single instant of genuine joy is possibly all that really counts at the end. And if taking that grab off a Trevor Barker goal ends up as my only remaining memory, I won't complain.

Some people kept the footy when it was kicked into the crowd and chucked a shitty one back instead. It was funny to watch the face of whichever player or umpire was waiting for the ball to come back over the fence. Concentrating on the game, they always took a few seconds to realise that a ring-in had been returned.

The Parking Lady

While cruising the Moorabbin side-streets one Saturday afternoon in search of a parking space, we saw a sign on a front lawn. Painted on the lid of an ice-cream container nailed to a wooden post (Mark had used this idea years earlier for an air-rifle target, before he discovered blackbirds), it simply stated: 'CARPARK — 50 CENTS'. We liked the price and the personal approach, so we became regulars for the remainder of that season.

Most of all, we liked the lady who lived there. In her early forties, she always dressed like those ultra-American wives who wait for their man to return from the moon: all head-scarves and over-sized sunglasses. She loved discussing the upcoming clashes and her knowledge of the Saints was boundless. We respected each other's ideas, and personally, I was thrilled to claim any kind of regular relationship with a woman.

Arriving for the first game of the following season, and taking care not to leave tyre marks on her gorgeous green grass, Sim parked the car, only to find we'd been presumptuous. The offer didn't apply this year. As Simon reversed the car, she ran after us: 'Listen, we get along well. How does one more season sound? Forget the fifty cents'. This delightful arrangement eventually came to an end when the Saints moved from Moorabbin. We never knew her name.

The sweet, musky aroma of wet autumn leaves was a sure sign the footy season was well underway. This was never more evident than when we waded though thousands of fallen red, orange and yellow leaves from the tram to the turnstiles at Princes Park. We took the tram from Elizabeth Street and watched old blokes hovering outside the dirty movie houses, trying to discover which deal offered better value. The Crazy Horse appeared to be popular. The only time we ever saw actual derro's hanging out in Melbourne was around Victoria Market as we purred past in those trams. They seemed fully trained in the art of 'How To Fight Yourself'.

Coming back, the tram was packed, giving anyone full o' beer the chance to pass wind without worry. To share bad air without being singled out must be a pleasure for some people. Once on board there was nowhere to go. In such situations, supporters of both sides had no choice but to stand among the odour, though never without complaint, 'Every Bloody Time' someone always shouted.

'Better out than in!' one fella philosophised.

At fourteen, I found these events fulfillng and even looked forward to the funny remarks a fart would warrant. It was infantile, yet as I laughed along with the others, I felt like one of the fellas. A man amongst men. I once attempted to join in by shouting 'Vince' after hearing an obvious honk. A man turned around as if he'd heard someone say his name. This reaction, combined with an obvious lack of laughter from anyone else, reminded me of how the term was probably only applicable among my schoolmates.

Years later, before the tram journey began, we wet the whistle at Young & Jackson's on the way, admiring Chloe's curves over a cold one. One year the Saints were at Princes Park on Anzac Day and as we arrived at Flinders Street station around midday, we saw Y&J's was packed. All the old Diggers use it as their local for the occasion because of the nearby march to the Shrine. One of the benefits for the old boys is that the younger generation show their respect by plying them with pots. So many elderly men getting pissed for free and all you could see and hear were body's dropping left, right and centre. Later in the day we observed the minute's silence before the game and seeing so many people with my eyes, yet hearing not a sound with my ears, always gave me the shivers.

The Bully

Where Mr Preece had failed in his efforts at delivering me a darn good hiding, Marvin Boondock succeeded. He was the tallest boy of our age in school and more a nasty than a naughty type. From the moment I sat at the desk in front of him in Mechanics, he had it in for me. Marvin looked like a hillbilly cowhand, more brute strength than brains. Imagine a less-bright version of Damian Monkhorst.

Initially, I rationalised that the constant clouts from behind were just horseplay, even though they bloody hurt, but I became more worried when he hit me harder each time we crossed paths in the corridor. I confided in a classmate, who offered the suggestion that I should put up or shut up. As I'd never been able to keep my mouth closed, I had no option. I was shit-scared, because he was a savage sort, but I'd recently discovered Bruce Lee in *Enter the Dragon* and I had a plan. As Marvin was too dense to knock down with my knuckles, I'd have to swing a foot towards his head and hope like hell. I took to wearing steel-capped black boots to school.

Syndal Tech had two ovals. One, known as 'up the back', was where the wayfarers hung out, sneaking smokes and maybe drinking a couple of cold cans, VB, UDL, whatever they could wrangle. The other was the 'main' oval, where the sports fans played footy with their friends. One lunchtime, Boondock and his band of bad guys decided to make the move from their base 'up the back' and cause mayhem on the main oval. They were in a particularly menacing mood. Basically, everyone playing football faced a flogging, as eight or so of these mean, mad bastards began bulldozing all the boys in sight. At sixteen, none of us minded a fight, but these blokes were out of control. A few of them grabbed Fonzie (thus christened for his surname — Flourentzou — and his leather jacket), held him by an arm and a leg and chucked him into the mud. This was frightening. We were being terrorised on our own turf.

As I watched all this, my adrenal glands went into overdrive. It was time to take action. Beckoning Marvin over, I heard myself say: 'Come here and have a go, you great galumph'. (Don't ask me what a galumph is. It just came out.) Not surprisingly, he found this most amusing. He attacked, henchmen hot on his heels, and I jumped, aiming my right foot at his jaw. As I missed, I fell flat on my back, and was not even allowed time to be embarrassed before being beaten into oblivion. Luckily, he didn't ever bother with me after that. He must have felt he'd made his point.

The Courtroom

Riding home from Fonzie's house around nine o'clock one summer night, I witnessed a fatal hit-and-run accident on the other side of the road. I didn't realise how football had furthered my education until I was later called to the witness stand in court. It was a terrible accident, and as the only bystander, I was determined not to be bamboozled by verbal dexterity.

'How far away were you when the incident occurred?', defence counsel demanded.

'Approximately forty metres', I answered.

'You've already testified as to your difficulty with mathematics at school. How can you be sure of the distances involved?' the barrister demanded cockily, raising an eyebrow.

'Because that's how far I can kick a footy', I replied with a smug smirk.

'I see', he said, visibly taken aback. 'No further questions, Your Honour.'

CHAPTER TWENTY

The Passion

During tight games, we were religious in our unshakeable faith in 'the boys'. If we were, say, three goals down in the final moments of the last quarter, the tribal element took over. There were games when it seemed that *every single person* in the outer and up in the grandstand was chanting: 'Saint Keel-dah' (clap, clap, clap), 'Saint Keel-dah' (clap, clap, clap).

The back wall of the corrugated-aluminium grandstand would echo and reverberate with the deafening roar. Somehow, I felt, if we each connected our hands hard enough together, with as much force as we could manage, and shouted as loud as our larynxes would allow, then the players just might understand how much we all *believed* in them. With the hairs standing up on the back of my neck, I'd survey the surrounding crowd with a sense of almost unbearable excitement. The intensity of our support must have seeped into the players' souls on occasion. We were *willing* them to win, to find another gear. It was audience participation in its purest form. Some players visibly responded to our rousing racket. It's worth recalling that not long ago, loyalty remained a valid football emotion. Robert Elphinstone wore number thirty-three, and put in for as many minutes each quarter. When the end was nigh and the Saints were in with a genuine chance, he and 'Joffa' Cunningham would run from one player to another, giving team-mates pep talks, trying to squeeze every last ounce of energy from their battle-weary bodies, perhaps as desperate for victory as were their success-starved supporters.

The fact that they were often simply outclassed by the opposition was beyond our control. You can only play as well as you're able. The English tolerate their cricket teams along these lines. Mates of ours who barracked for other teams occasionally joined us behind the goals at Moorabbin. Some hoped to offer witty retorts to the notorious insult-merchants among us. Some were too scared to say a word, either for their side or against ours. Every one of them remarked upon the way St Kilda supporters at Moorabbin seemed able to assist the Saints jump higher, chase harder and kick longer, through the force of our collective *will*, presented in the form of a wall of sound. One mate called it a 'home *crowd* advantage', the sheer force of which effectively put a wind beneath the players' wings. We were only too aware of the futility of attempting to cheer the ball between the sticks. No, it was the human element we enjoyed trying to influence. The ball wouldn't travel further or more accurately once it had left the boot, but before it had, we had a chance to inspire the player to the point where he might kick it further or straighter.

Supporters of other sides were able to sense how much our team meant to us. It impressed and intimidated in equal parts. Our furious fervour was such that they couldn't fail to weigh their own level of commitment against ours. The scales nearly always tipped in our favour. Opposing players often admitted as much during after-match interviews. If we weren't able to take pride in winning then at least we could take pride in how much we *wanted* to. By 'want', I mean want, like a pregnant woman wants pickled onions at three in the morning. I mean want, like a just-released long-term prisoner wants sex. I mean want, as in have to have. I don't mean decided want, I mean compulsive want, instinctive want, gut want. Want like a shark wants to attack the vibrations a swimmers legs generate in its nerve endings. Want. Crave. Desire. Need. Demand. Want.

Loyal supporters gain a lot more than premiership cups, whether their side succeeds or fails. Watching Tony Lockett over the years — his senior debut when he scored a goal with his first kick; his starring performances for the State side; the first time he topped the ton — gave Simon and me an almost parental pleasure. We watched St Kilda slowly but surely improve to the point where at last, after twelve long years, one of our dreams came true: a finals appearance.

The Dressing Rooms

Following St Kilda home victories, a crowd would gather outside the dressing-room door to personally salute the stars, slap them on the back, and generally indulge in a bit of hero-worship. These men were our gods. No doubt it was annoying, but for a lowly club like St Kilda, putting up with it was essential to maintaining any sort of supporter base. If they wanted us to attend each week, they had to accept the occasional outpouring of passion. The doorman quickly assessed each attempt at entry, instantly recognising past players and male relatives of team members. The rest of us could only smile sweetly and hope.

A rare win made us want to experience victory at close quarters, sing the club song with the team, smell the sweat, watch in wonder as the players savoured their success. Once in a while, mainly at Moorabbin, they let us into the inner sanctum. Most supporters afforded this favour stayed on the outskirts, acting almost as if they were in church. Motivational mottoes adorned the walls, numbered lockers bore the names of past and present players, and the eucalyptus-oil smell of the rub-downs (perhaps the definitive football-club fragrance) permeated everything. If a TV camera crew was filming an interview, kids would crowd around in the background, trying to get their face in the frame — probably the same kids who sat near the fence, waving for the telly whenever the ball went out of bounds in front of them. Interviews were often interrupted as the subject copped half an orange in the ear from an excitable team-mate.

One day, Simon and I saw a roster on the dressing-room wall. It listed each senior players' post-match responsibilities, telling each member of the team exactly where they were supposed to hang around for an hour after the game! Hefty fines applied to anyone disregarding this PR requirement.

Each club has separate sects of supporters, all contributing cash in various ways throughout the season. St Kilda has The Sinners and The Haloes, among other cliques of this kind. Each sect has its separate area within the club's walls, where they gather as a group. Understandably, these people expect some attention from the footballers they're financing. The club therefore ensures that they can rub shoulders with the stars, and occasionally, have their opinions heard.

Like Simon and me, the sponsors simply wanted a sense of involvement. It's just that, unlike the rest of us, they can't be dismissed when delivering a load of old drunken dribble. Performance isn't always enough. Forget about the boss's barbie and he may forget about you. From the bar to the boardroom to the centre bounce, politics play a part in the whole process.

The Sponsors

Being short on success equalled minimal television coverage. Minimal television coverage equalled scant interest from sponsors. In what must've been a desperate effort to woo some wealth, St Kilda once allowed the bloke who played the gendarme in the Yoplait Yogurt ads to stand on the ground at the start of a game and toss the coin for the opposing captains. Not surprisingly, it didn't work.

The best financial deal the Saints negotiated during the 1980s was with a famous greeting-card company. The problems arose when the logo was sewn onto the players' on-field outfits, particularly when we played the Magpies. Collingwood was sponsored by Yakka, in keeping with the club's working-class tradition. It was harder for the Saints players to look intimidating when they took the field, the word 'Valentine' glowing red on their guernseys.

A more appropriate sponsor was Hugall and Hoyle, the hose-fitting manufacturers. St Kilda gained a deserved reputation for watering down the ground on the Friday night before matches at Moorabbin. This was done on the theory that if our team was slow and sloppy, a wet surface would tend to bring the opposition down towards our level. At least scores would be lower and losing margins less embarrassing. It must've seemed easier than becoming a better side. The results show that we continued to lose the majority of our games, be they in wet conditions or dry, at home or away, so the procedure was pointless anyway.

Collingwood's Tony Shaw, for one, spoke out not only against the ground's mud-pie complexion, he also criticised the freezing-cold showers, claiming he'd rather drive home covered in mud than wash himself at Moorabbin. Then again, if rumours reaching the suburbs were correct, I suspect he didn't have the same reason to be shy in the showers as I did when playing for the Nottinghill Bs.

Victoria Park

Victoria Park was the only ground where we feared for our lives. During Tommy Hafey's days as coach, Collingwood had cheer squads at *both* ends of the ground. The locals also took pride in infiltrating the only area where we, the opposition supporters, were allowed to stand. They stood among us like Magpie police, threatening anybody rash enough to speak out against their team. One man-mountain had a shaven head, wore jet-black wrap-around shades and stood about six feet six. He sported an ankle-length jacket, the type in which bank robbers conceal pump-action shotguns, a red-back spider tattoo on his skull and a Fu Manchu-style moustache. The sweet-smelling aroma of marijuana seeped from his hand-rolled cigarettes.

Collingwood thrashed St Kilda whenever we visited Victoria Park. In Round Four of 1979, the Pies kicked thirty-one goals to our three and had fifty-two shots at goal to our fourteen! It was the second game Simon and I had ever attended. It was difficult to watch our team being beaten this badly, but at Victoria Park, we weren't even able to console ourselves by abusing the opposition, unless we were feeling suicidal enough about the game to risk serious injury. Fu Manchu and his mates came along for a fight rather than to follow a footy game. Their verbal contributions to the action made it apparent that they knew few of their own players. Even the score was beyond them on some occasions.

With the help of Scott, the intellectual of our group of Saints supporters, we finally worked out a way to enjoy ourselves at Victoria Park. As the majority of hard-men Magpie supporters seemed to be educationally challenged (in other words, thick), we simply expanded our vocabulary. It became an art form to insult a Collingwood player without their scary supporters realising it. Thus, Ronnie Wearmouth became an 'imbecile', Billy Picken was 'tedious', Ricky Barham's efforts were 'atrocious', and the entire team gave out a 'noxious stench'.

Shane from Syndal Tech

Like certain Saints players before and since, Shane was nearly lost to the St Kilda Social Club. Accepting an invitation inside one afternoon, he was impressed by the well-dressed women and the table service. Simon and I were upset by what we saw as a defection. We said as much. Shane accused us of jealousy, though I deny it to this day. I had perfectly good reasons for rejecting such trappings. Firstly, they wanted you to wear a tie in there. For me, adjusting a tie in the mirror before a football match is unimaginable. Secondly, the game is watched from behind glass. I like to feel the atmosphere, the mood of the moment, that split second of silence as someone soars for a screamer, the roar as he brings it down, the bad vibe during an all-in-brawl, the raw fury at an outrageous umpiring decision. These things cannot be experienced in a closed-off room. You may as well be watching on TV. How could an umpire or opposition player hope to hear your abuse from in there? We often saw the windows shaking as members punched the glass at moments of high drama. I saw this as a subconscious escape attempt, a desire to be outside amongst it all. Thirdly, of course, nobody had ever invited me in. After four or five home games, the novelty wore off. Shane was back in the outer, where he belonged.

Simon collected *Football Records* for several seasons, getting maximum value for money on match day before storing them away, if possible spotless and uncreased. Sim was cool and calm in most environments, but the footy wasn't one of them. He regularly cut himself in the head as he raised his fists in triumph or temper, forgetting he had a pen in his hand. Drip, drip, went the blood, off his temple and onto his *Football Record*, shocking him as the first bright-red droplet sullied the page.

In his *Football Record*, Sim recorded every score for the full four quarters. It was humiliating if an opposition player kicked so many goals that there wasn't enough room to mark them all down in the space provided. The *Record* was also handy for checking the selected sides as they ran out onto the ground, ticking off names as each player appeared out of the race. Just as Australia occasionally sprung a surprise by using Craig McDermott to open the batting in one-day games, footy clubs throw blokes in out of nowhere once in a while as well. This is hugely exciting, because it makes you think there's a secret plan. Hawthorn tried this trick in the 1985 grand final, when David O'Halloran came in for his first game of the season, only to be slaughtered by Essendon spearhead Paul Salmon.

The Impostor

During the mid to late 1980s, when St Kilda Football Club was floundering financially, management came up with an offer to pay all debtors twenty-two (or seven for some) cents in the dollar. Those willing to accept would be guaranteed payment up front, while those wanting everything owed would have to wait and see if it ever became available. Luckily (for the fans), the deal was done. Supporters raised funds through diverse schemes. But, as the old saying goes, there's always one bad apple that spoils the bunch, and in this case, the bloke arrested for impersonating Trevor Barker was it. A convicted confidence trickster, he faced charges in court for taking advantage of the Victorian sporting public's proud record of opening their wallets to save their traditional footy teams.

Operating mainly in Moorabbin and surrounding suburbs, the villain knocked on numerous doors, wearing a St Kilda tracksuit top and pretending to be Trevor Barker. I'd tried the last part myself, for my photo album, but never for nicking money from old ladies. Barker was St Kilda captain at the time, had twice won the club's 'Best and Fairest' award, and played for the State. Being one of Barker's more fanatical fans, I was just as upset at the people who fell for the scam as I was with the culprit. How could they make such a mistake? Didn't *everybody* know Trevor Barker? I was incensed. Anyone that ignorant almost *deserved* to be ripped off.

CHAPTER TWENTY-ONE

Brownlow Night

Dad accepted Victorian Premier John Cain's early retirement scheme and took Mum overseas on the proceeds, leaving me with the house to myself. Their departure led to general mayhem and misbehaviour, but it's Brownlow night 1987 that remains in my memory. I'd arranged for a few friends to come around on Brownlow night, traditionally the Monday before the grand final, and everyone was to bring some booze. We intended to make a top night of the telecast. Tony Lockett had kicked the ton and was one of the season's stars, though curiously, with a month to go, few in the media fancied his Brownlow chances: *The Sun* quoted a Darwin bookmaker as offering fifteen to one. These odds were so outrageous that Simon and I decided to have two hundred each on him.

As betting on the Brownlow was illegal in Victoria and at least up for discussion in other States, we set about finding a bookie to place our bet. The sporting journalists from *The Sun* were reticent when asked for a phone number, and we began to believe that the infamous

Darwin bookies were the invention of desperate editors keen to claim they had connections. Finally, an anonymous call came through with the inside information and we managed to contact the bookie mentioned in the press. Wanting to put our money where our mouths were, we endured one excuse after another until his odds came down so far it was futile. Instead, the exercise cost us almost two hundred bucks in phone bills, just to discover what a pathetic prick that Darwin bookie was. Had his original odds ever existed, Simon and I would each have won three thousand. Not that I'm bitter.

Tony Lockett had already achieved cult status among most male football followers. More than any full forward before him, he combined rare scoring skills with a rugged ruthlessness. If a full back hung on unfairly, Lockett hit 'em hard. He was an angry young man in no mood for mischief. They were warned once and then went down. It was obvious to me that Lockett was not an only child, as many of his disciplinary tactics came straight from the *Big Brother Textbook of Torture*:

Step 1: Get your sibling on the ground.

Step 2: Sit on his/her chest and pin his/her arms down with your knees.

Step 3: Proceed with punishment.

Footscray's Ricky Kennedy was on the receiving end of one particular pounding during which I half-expected him to produce a sign on a stick, saying 'Help!'. Sydney Swans defender Rod Carter nearly lost his nickname — 'Tilt' — after Lockett hammered his hang-to-the-left head so hard, it straightened up for a second and almost stayed that way. North Melbourne's Mick Martyn gave as good as he got on most occasions, but even he once surfaced from a Plugger headlock looking like a man with sunburn using chilli sauce as a soothing lotion. One afternoon at Victoria Park, I'd swear I saw Plugger giving Ronnie McKeown a Chinese burn. The man was magnificent.

Tony Lockett had a sensational season. Round Four saw us lose to Melbourne whilst I was in the midst of glandular fever. (Apparently, this ailment is also known as 'the kissing disease', which considering my poor record in this area, confirmed me as very unlucky.) It knocked me so rotten that I almost didn't make the game, which was unheard of and would've made me feel even sicker, as I'd have missed Plugger kick a then club-record twelve goals.

Round Nineteen was also particularly memorable. Part of Dad's planning for the overseas adventure was to appear unannounced on the doorstep of his younger brother in England. They'd been apart thirty-seven years. Two weeks before Mum and Dad's departure, I answered the phone to a Pommy voice that was asking for the old man. 'It's your Uncle Gerald,' he announced, 'your dad's brother. Can I have a word with him? I've just arrived at Tullamarine'. Dad's plans to spring a surprise had been thwarted — Gerald had the same idea, a little earlier. After thirty-seven years, they'd made the same plans, without consultation, within a fortnight of each other. It certainly took the gloss of Dad's big surprise, but as it was, he got to see his brother sooner than expected.

So when my parents took their trip, as planned, they left Gerald, with two weeks remaining in Australia, in the tender care of his nephews. He was a fine fella, for a Pommy. Fortunately he enjoyed a drink, and on the eve of Round Nineteen, with Plugger sitting pretty on ninety-three goals, we took Gerald out on the town, as it happened to be his final night in Australia. We began by introducing him to Chloe at Young & Jackson's, and moved on to the Sherlock Holmes, where he was free to prepare for home by drinking pints of Guinness. Though in his fifties, Uncle Gerald drank Mark, Simon and me firmly under the table. Back at our place, he introduced us to — and soundly beat us at — a succession of English drinking games, so it was a sick and sorry Simon and I who arrived at Moorabbin the next day, having earlier sent our uncle, looking his age, in a taxi to Tullamarine airport. Gerald was lucky Mum and Dad were still overseas — he was certainly in no state for Mum's tea-towel farewell!

Our opponent that day, Footscray, was in the five, but I was confident, as we'd won four in a row, and I couldn't remember the last time that had occurred. The game was in the balance as Trevor Barker cleared from defence and Alex Marcou, via a couple of handpasses, targeted Tony Lockett with one of his perfect passes. Bullseye. Plugger, on ninety-nine, lines up, kicks straight, and has his hundred goals.

The highlight of actually being there when somebody kicks their hundredth goal of the season was less the witnessing of an awesome achievement than the chance to run onto the ground *during* a game. (We'd done it when opposition full forwards had achieved the feat playing St Kilda: with Quinlan, in 1984, and again when Brian Taylor was given a phantom free kick by umpire Peter Cameron, in 1986. Taylor injured himself with only one goal to get, and has since confessed that Cameron guaranteed a free kick to get him the hundredth. Taylor's opponent, Danny Frawley, was furious.) Somehow it felt more special than running onto the ground *after* a game. It was almost as if we were playing a part in proceedings, when in fact we were merely interrupting them.

Once in a while, you could get on between the reserves and the seniors and have a kick in front of a big crowd but such occasions were rare. When it did happen, there'd be blokes trying to sit on each other's shoulders all over the shop, seeking attention. Army Reserve Cup games on Sundays at the Lakeside Oval were even better, because you could have a kick on the ground at quarter-time and then stand around the huddle to hear the coach's address. To see the players sweating and hear them swearing at such close range was to be allowed unequalled access to a club's core. These games were also unique in that the players could be heard talking to each other as the play took place.

A fat bloke with dyed-blond hair who thought he was Mark Harvey was shown on telly each week, having a kick at half-time in his Essendon jumper, shorts and socks. Although I thought he was obviously soft in the head, I sadly considered dressing up as Trevor Barker and kicking his arse competitively.

The crowd cleared from the ground (Simon can be seen on the video of that game, in slow motion, if you know where to look, lurching towards Lockett through the throng and offering his warm, half-empty can of beer, a congratulory gesture on which Tony took a raincheck), and not long afterwards, with the Saints three points behind, Plugger snared his eighth for the day. It was also the winning goal, the one that put us three points in front at the final siren and put Footscray out of the five.

We couldn't imagine Plugger allowing his boss to berate him, his neighbour to annoy him or anyone to honk their horn at him in traffic, as we mere mortals had to. In the outer, we had no complaints concerning his constant suspensions. We thought the aggression an essential element of his game. As he grew older, he proved otherwise.

Interestingly, a reserve-grade fixture swap that day saw the Under 19s play the curtain-raiser to the main game. We turned up early to watch Wayne Bulte, my Little League team-mate with Trevor Barker's birthday, line up alongside Shane Warne, who was playing for the Saints. They got done badly that day, which no doubt prompted our current-day cricketing legend to concentrate solely on his bowling.

The Brownlow count began. As we lay around the lounge room, cracking open cold cans, Lockett steadily compiled a towering tally until, nearing the end, he shared top spot with Hawthorn's John Platten. Surely a rover known as 'The Rat' couldn't ruin this rare chance of a St Kilda celebration. By any measure of success, we'd endured a devastating drought. As Ross Oakley prepared to reveal the votes from the final round, we cracked open four bottles of Brownlow Port, purchased from Mr Bedalis' bottle shop around the corner. Its label featured the actual medal on the front, photographed in full colour, and a list of past winners on the back. Our mood was vibrant, there was beer in abundance and we'd come to a conclusion. Should Lockett win, we would move on to Moorabbin and run amok.

In the end, it was a tie. As intoxicated by the outcome as by the alcohol, we erupted into a scene of absolute uproar — dancing, hugging, clinking glasses, and playing the St Kilda theme song so loud it was distorted beyond recognition. Plugger delivered a suitably shambolic speech and I obeyed an urge to run down the main road clad only in a sleeveless St Kilda jumper I'd slipped on to show my allegiance. A cab was called and we made our way to Moorabbin, where we found the social club in a state of disarray. The doorman said he would allow almost anything, due to the occasion, but trying to enter in sleeveless jumper and a pair of jocks was beyond a joke. As some restaurants provide ties for tardy customers, the doorman produced a pair of pants, which he said would see me through.

It wasn't long before the man of the hour arrived with Danny Frawley and Nicky Winmar, the triumphant trio resplendent in tuxedos and cummerbunds. Lockett was mobbed within moments. Simon and I got him in a bear hug from both sides, kissing a cheek each as somebody took a snapshot. We hadn't hesitated; he hadn't hit us. The world was wonderful. Lockett was loving it. He even signed our friend's forehead with a big black texta. Shrugging everyone aside, he announced an open bar, with him picking up the bill. This was a generous gesture, considering *we* had come to buy *him* a beer, but I didn't hear anybody argue.

Measuring the mood, Shane took the opportunity to snuggle up to a ravishing redhead. Things looked to be going quite well for him until suddenly, and with only seconds to spare, he stepped away and spewed into his St Kilda tracksuit top, which he'd taken off just in time to catch the carrots. She was put somewhat off, but didn't take it personally.

One week later, Mum and Dad returned from overseas, in time for Simon and Lisa's October wedding. It was all just as Lisa had predicted.

The Lover

My lack of success with the ladies remained. I had a mate named Barry Barnaby who looked like Shaggy out of *Scooby Doo*, though he hated any mention made of it. His sister was supposedly keen on me. I'd never met her which didn't matter because any girl who looked like Barry could never be in contention. Pass me the forty-foot pole. Plus, everyone I knew left their mate's sisters' alone. An unspoken rule. Just my luck.

I'd discovered 'self-pleasure' at a late age, previously taking the insult 'wanker' to be a literal description of the victim's permanent sexual standing. I believed a wanker to be somebody who, after many years and varied attempts at finding themselves a lover, had conceded defeat forever. Not me. I intended to persevere. Then I overheard a pub discusson, during which a series of very funny, if overly graphic tales were told among several drunken males. It became apparent that either the blokes I was listening to were evildoers, or that I had the wrong end of the stick. So to speak. It seemed there was no shame in the whole scenario. I decided then and there to have an early night. The result reminded me of an ad campaign at the time.

'Nibble Nobbies Nuts – Once You've Started, You Just Can't Stop'. It was an out-of-this-world experience, even better than touching a transistor battery onto the tip of my tongue. I couldn't believe I'd not known about it earlier. All that time alone. Wasted. The combination of unemployment and my failure so far to attract the female species, ensured there was plenty of opportunity for me to catch up. Eventually, Mum made mention of the ever-increasing pile of 'used' tissues shoved down the side of my bed. She being a woman and me being thick, I assumed my special male secret was safe and cleared them away without embarrassment. I didn't think about what alternative explanations may have crossed her mind.

'My son must have the runniest nose in the country'.

Nor did I wonder what she made of the 'Ripper '76' compilation album cover by my bedside, which served as a kick-start to proceedings with its 'girl-wearing-ripped-denim' design.

Masturbation was a revelation but still the problem persisted. Getting laid. When the drought broke, it broke big.

I arrived at 'Derbys Nitespot' in Caulfield, already drunk from celebrating St Kilda's fifth win on the trot and Lockett's hundredth goal, both that very afternoon. The way Derbys deliberately mis-spelt 'Nitespot' in neon was considered cool. I'd recently turned eighteen and for a brief period, Derbys was first choice on a Saturday night. 'Area' night-club in Croydon had been a bad experience, somehow I always copped a smack in the mouth without any obvious motive. 'Stage One' was closer to home but it's revolving dance floors rarely agreed with a stomach full of Southern Comfort and 'KTs' in Knox had refused me entry ever since an unsavoury suggestion I'd allegedly made in the direction of one of their dancers. Soaked to the skin this particular Saturday evening, from a run in the pouring rain, I was allowed entry to Derbys with relative ease. If the bouncers were in a belligerent mood, a situation often fuelled by a night of fights, it could be bedlam. Queues around the corner, no blokes let in without a bird, shirt with collar essential, sorry mate but not in those shoes sort of stuff. Usually stepping out of a cab with a few other fellas, we tried every trick in the book.

Approaching incoming girls around the corner and offering a few free drinks if they'd hold our hand past the door patrol. Breaking up into two-man teams. Attempting re-entry in disguise. Swapping jackets, transforming hairstyles or both, after an initial knockback. Waiting an hour or so for the changing of the guard. There were many ruses. Desperate for a drink and raring for a root, one way or another we always ended up inside. So on this occasion I was six steps beyond the pay-in desk, when a pretty girl on a bar stool pulled me toward her for a pash. The flourescent stamp on my wrist was still wet and already I was doing well. The DJ played the same old shit. 'Oh what a night. Late December back in sixty-three...'

My hair absorbed the stink of cigarette smoke which would make me dry-reach the next morning when the water hit my head in the shower. But for now, what did I care? This tasty blonde had her tongue in my mouth and we hadn't even formally met yet. Behind me I heard the final crack of the white ball sinking black on the pool table. Above it hung a cheapshit shiny-black-framed protrait, showing Bogart, Presley and Monroe, shooting the breeze against a backroom bar.

'Boom Boom Boom, Let's go back to my room...'

Doesn't this bloke buy any new bloody records?, I wondered as my new friend released her lip-lock, giving me a good look at her face for the first time. She was pretty. Porcelain doll pretty.

'Do you wanna?' she said, slurring slightly.

'Do I wanna what?' I asked, knowing she wanted a dance and planning to politely suggest where she could stick that idea.

'Boom Boom! Go back to my room?' she answered.

I almost shit myself. I'd been offering my virginity to any woman who wanted it for what seemed like forever. Happy to get my hand down a girl's pants on a good night, I was suddenly offered the ultimate event on a platter.

The cabbie woke us when we reached the destination he was given, scribbled on the back of a beer mat in eyeliner. She got out first. The driver winked, wished me luck and handed me my change as Rick Astley faded in and out of frequency on his car stereo.

After an agonising wait on the doorstep, we were inside and heading down a long dark corridor. Whispering, she told me to open the door at the end while she went for a wee. I had to stop myself from doing that dance we all do at one point of our lives, alone. In awe and celebraton of what we are about to, or what we have just achieved. My hand held in a giggle. I'm about to leave my boyhood behind, I thought.

Jesaulenko! You beauty!

I weaved my way toward the door. The closer I got, the further it was away. I held the handle and heard the hinges creak as if they were connected to an amplifier. Failing to find the light switch, I edged toward the middle of the room, took a risk and was relieved to feel a mattress beneath me as I let my bottom lead my body toward the floor in a falling motion.

Lucy (She'd introduced herself while waiting to collect her coat from the cloakroom) soon joined me and I saw her silhouette begin to get undressed. I'd been bluntly invited back to her bed and was now in the darkened boudoir of this luxuriant lady, early of hour and full of alcohol. I knew why but it never occurred to me that she would openly admit it! Is this the way it works? No having to sneak my arm around her waist while causing a distraction by complimenting her on the curtains? No need for excuses such as 'I'm sorry for taking my shoes off but my feet are hurting'?

No cups of coffee?

It was too easy. Like those pens you turn upside down to make the lady's clothes come off.

The whole scene made me nervous. Scared, in fact. She slipped under the sheets and advised me to disrobe and do the same. I was happy she'd left the lights off. She wouldn't see my bony body. My eyes adjusted enough to see her breasts' transform as she lay back and let gravity go to work. I was amazed to discover each boob's depth diminish, while at the same time increasing in circumference. Either way she was well stacked. For a fleeting moment my mind raced back to that second screen at the drive-in.

We were now side by side, facing each other. Kissing. Caressing. My blood was flowing fine. No brewers droop. I'd heard blokes talking about the effects of too many beers but that worry was out of the way. She rolled us together so I ended up on top.

Here we go, here we go, here we go!

Then disaster struck.

Hang on a minute, I thought. It must be around here somewhere. I was having more trouble gaining entry than she'd had at the front door with her key.

"Hang on a minute".

Oh no, I said it out loud.

What's more, my manhood was now rapidly reducing.

'Relax', she said in a soothing voice. It was no use. I was trying to play snooker with a rope. Suddenly, a cough come from another room! My dick disppeared. Like a snail's eye when you touch it with a fingertip. This was a scene I'd not envisaged whenever I saw Trevor Barker going home after a game with a luscious, lip-gloss laden lady. Surely this wasn't the way things worked. What was I doing wrong?

'Don't tell me you're a weird one?' I heard Lucy say, snapping my drifting mind back into the moment.

'What? Whattaya mean, a weird one?' I asked, defensively.

'Maybe you need something kinky to get you going' she suggested, chin down and looking at me cheekily from under her eyebrows.

'Kinky?'

'Yeah, you know, maybe you want me to wear something sexy, or strange, to start things up again?'

Then and there an idea hit me like the blinding bright light of a sunset through the windscreen. Through the glare I fished around among my discarded clothes for the St Kilda jumper I always wore beneath any outfit, in the hope an extra layer might disguise my skinnyness.

'Why don't you wear this and we'll see how we go?' I answered, slinging the Saints colours in her direction.

She slipped it on and we were back on track. The going was good until mid-way, when we repositioned ourselves. With Lucy now on all fours, facing away from me and still with the guernsey on, I was confronted with her long blonde hair hanging above the No.1 sewn on the back. Planning to get some purchase, she then reached her arms up in the air, so as to grip the top edge of the headboard. We'd not met before but something about this image seemed familiar.

'BARKER!'

I heard Peter Landy in my head.

The snail's eye shrank again.

'What's the matter?' she enquired, a mix of desire and disappointment to her tone.

'You wouldn't understand' I muttered, pretty much to myself, before falling into a fitful sleep.

I had one leg out of the window when she woke up.

'What are you doing?' she asked with an incredulous inflection.

'I, I, I, I'm not sure' I said, which was a lie. I was absolutely certain. 'A runner' was the real answer.

I was too gutless to tell the truth. Which was, that I was too cowardly to face her, as the embarrassment of my earlier incompetence seemed magnified in the morning light. No, my only option was to escape. More to the point, I wanted to avoid meeting any member of her family. What did I know of her? The more I recalled the cough I had heard in my mind, the more convinced I was that it came from some heavy, hairy, muscular madman.

What would I say?

'Wait here a minute and I'll get my brother to give you a lift' she said, to my dismay.

Her brother? She must be joking. It sounded more like an order than an offer. I prepared myself to be a human punch-bag.

So out she went and I waited. And waited ... and waited. Then I waited some more. I could have watched the grand final on video while I waited. There came a knock on the door, followed by muffled laughter.

'Hello?' I said softly.

A bloke barged in. 'Shaggy!' Obviously, his sister had given up waiting for him to introduce us.

The Day Job

I was employed at this time at the Reserve Bank Of Australia in Collins Street, as a Counterfeit Surveillance Officer. In other words, I was a poorly paid clerk. While the job filled my parents with pride, I'm certain it shocked the neighbours and most of my friends' folks, all of whom had begun to treat me with the type of condescension such a lazy, long-term layabout deserved. Mum and Dad had taken to leaving the *Waverley Gazette* open at the employment pages, with various vacancies circled in red ink. Having deliberately applied for jobs which either didn't exist or were way above my station, I was shocked to receive two offers of employment on the one day. Unfortunately, Mum had taken both calls, so there was no escape. My parents' sense of relief was palpable as I announced my decision at the kitchen table: 'I reckon the bank offers a brighter future than mowing lawns for Waverley Council, so I suppose I'd better get myself a suit.'

The Reserve Bank is basically a storeroom where vans pick up and drop off the dollars. Lots of dollars. My task was to run fistfuls of notes through a machine, which checked for length, width, watermark and metallic strip. It was not uncommon for fifty million bucks to pass through my hands in a day.

I was surprised to discover that a gold bar the size of an Eskimo Pie weighs the same as a house brick. I also learned that if Alle de Wolde had *actually* been worth his weight in gold, then at $470 an ounce, his 88 kilos (3800 ounces) was worth $1,457,000. Which, in 1979, could have bought the entire Scanlen's footy card company, and still left enough to buy a new duffle-coat.

Entering the Reserve Bank each day saw me endure security measures like those Maxwell Smart negotiates during the opening credits of *Get Smart* episodes. There were solid steel doors and iron bars all over the shop. I was sacked after displaying what was described as 'a general lack of interest'. They were wrong there. I was interested alright — not in the work, but in figuring out a way to drink with Ronnie Biggs on a Brazilian beach. Such a monotonous job involving so much money meant I was always wondering how to flee with a fortune. I wouldn't have had the balls to pull off any plan and I didn't have the brains to conceive a blueprint, but it was a top way to kill time. The distraction of dreaming of what I'd do with my newfound wealth must've been obvious from the faraway look in my eyes.

CHAPTER TWENTY-TWO

The Girl

Shane, who was moving up the ranks of the Gas and Fuel Corporation, once threw a spanner in the works by bringing a girl along to a game.

Unlike me and the majority of my other mates, Shane had a personal plan. Having left Syndal Tech early to become a plumber and gasfitter, he was doing well and, by the time he turned eighteen, owned a top-quality Commodore with all the trimmings. John Farnham's *You're the Voice* was a huge hit, as was his accompanying haircut, as far as Shane was concerned. My feathered Warwick Capper look suddenly faced stiff competition. *Miami Vice* was top-rating telly at the time, so Shane and I used to hit the suburban dance floors dressed in the show's sharp style. Shane was Don Johnson and I was, well, Don Johnson: grey, flecked sports jackets worn over pastel-coloured T-shirts. Smart casual, as it said on the disco door. Shane successfully used this ensemble to get girls, while I, wearing the same outfit, was universally ignored by the fairer sex.

Who brings a girl to a game? An all-male group behind the goals meant we could say what we wanted without much fear of offending anybody. I am able to swear in front of my Father, but would never dare drop four-letter words around my Mum. Nowadays, that attitude is considered sexist, but in my limited experience of women at the time, it seemed safer not to swear too much in their company. Men, in contrast, never seemed to notice. I was always fascinated to hear well-dressed businessmen in bars or on buses, swearing like a brickkie's labourer. The footy being a public domain, our male-bonding area was often infiltrated by large numbers of unsuspecting women. These occasions saw a lower level of bad language, but deleting our expletives prevented us from letting fly in our customary manner. They drink in our bars, earn equal incomes — where will it all end?!

So Shane should have known better. Worse, his girlfriend didn't want to know about the game. Instead, she made constant small talk regarding music, movies and generally anything but football, all while we were trying to watch the match. This type of discussion is fine, of course, in any normal social environment, but standing room in the outer amongst a crowd of footy fanatics is definitely not a normal social environment. To appreciate a game, I need to concentrate for the entire two hours. The League, in the interests of enticing families to the footy, has taken measures to ensure that, as the years go by, our style of supporter becomes the minority. Hooray, some may say, but where does that leave us, the last of the knuckleheads? It's the fanatics, after all, who pour much-needed cash into club coffers, win, lose or draw.

Steve the Postie took leave from our group to spend a couple of seasons in the grandstand. His dad had developed a renewed interest in footy, and wanted to take the weight off his feet away from the drunks. It made sense to us, and he hadn't gone behind glass, so Steve was spared our taunts. Steve was the only bloke I knew who rode a motorbike, and not just for work. His dad coming along to the games was something of a relief, because it meant Steve went straight home after the game, instead of having a kick with us. Leigh Matthews-like in his style, Steve left us with many a headache after he ploughed unexpectedly through a pack.

Young Jason veered off only when puberty reared its ugly head. His hormones took hold, and within weeks he was missing matches to play tennis with a 'babe' he'd met on the school bus. Throughout all this, Simon and I were immovable. Our interest was terminal, whether we liked it or not.

The Nudity

My streak down the main road on Brownlow night revived the adrenaline rush I'd experienced when Helen Demenico ran starkers onto the MCG in 1982. Just as a childhood experience of fire apparently inspires many an adult arsonist, I seemed to have been influenced by that earlier event. It couldn't have been exhibitionism, because I was ashamed of my skinny frame, but somewhere along the line, I became a streakaholic.

Simon's buck's night, conducted while Mum and Dad were still overseas, had concluded at seven in the morning at Caulfield racecourse. Reeling out of Derbys Nitespot, we'd decided it would be a great idea to watch the thoroughbreds being put through their paces. The track was empty.

Simon and I had stayed the distance, along with one other survivor, Dick Peddle, the middle Peddle brother. Chef, former student at Syndal Tech and certifiable madman, he challenged us to a naked sprint down the straight. We selected a place on the last corner, disrobed and were off. Picture the scene. Sunday morning, Caulfield racecourse. The sun is shining. Three grown men sprint naked down the straight after a solid night's drinking. As we reached the halfway mark, a racket started somewhere above us. Tradesmen working silently on the grandstand were clattering their tools against the girders. 'Have a look at this!' we heard from on high. 'I've heard of the Cox Plate, but this is ridiculous'.

Two years later, I went with a bunch of other blokes to watch a mutual mate play in a District Cricket Association final. Victorian players are plucked from these teams, so it was a top-class contest. University versus Carlton. Carlton was batting on the final day and had been stonewalling all afternoon, slowly sapping the strength of Josh Marquet, our opening-bowler mate. The game was at the Junction Oval. It was my first visit there since I'd seen Quinlan kick the ton for the Roy Boys, and this, combined with the maudlin effects of one too many beers, brought back fond memories. Sick of waiting for one team or the other to grab the game by the scruff of the neck, I snapped out of my melancholy mood and decided to stir things up a bit. Craig Bradley, Carlton Football Club's star recruit from Port Adelaide and also a quality cricketer, was at the crease as I sprinted across the pitch without a stitch on. The crowd went wild. I jumped back over the fence and ran for the safety of a nearby park. Puffed out and pumped full of freedom, I pulled my board shorts (which I'd carried across the pitch) back on, lay on a bench and got my breath back.

In the next over, University took two vital wickets and went on to win the match. I was sent for — the lucky mascot. A week-long free-beer celebration led to Luna Park, where I was at it again, this time getting out of my seat on the Ghost Train and standing in the dark by a skeleton that lit up as each carriage rounded the corner. After the part where they felt the spiders' legs tickling the tops of their heads, people in the oncoming cars were terrified by my bare bot!

You had to be there.

These antics were unplanned. In time, my desire to undress at public venues declined. Why it stopped is as much a mystery to me as why it started.

The Final Five

Towards the end of the 1987 season, Melbourne was marching towards the finals and their finesse-laden captain, Robbie Flower, was on fire. In the final round, the

Saints were playing the Eagles in Perth on the Sunday, so on Saturday, I went to the Western Oval to see if the Dees could notch up the win over Footscray required to make the final five. Melbourne and Footscray, along with St Kilda, formed a hopeless trio that had occupied the lower rungs of the ladder for as long as I'd been following football, so there was a wave of public support behind the Demons' run towards the finals.

The negative side of fanatically following a footy team is that you're rarely able to watch any others. While Tony Lockett was a benefit of watching the Saints every week, the burden was that we never saw much of Jason Dunstall. I honestly believe Plugger to be the better player, but Dunstall has been such a magnificent player over so many years, I'd like to have seen more of him, so as to form a fair opinion.

This, however, was one of the rare occasions when I went to a game in which my team was not involved. Not supporting either side, I hoped to enjoy the game in a relaxed manner, reasoning that without allegiance, I could not be upset by any umpiring decisions. However, with St Kilda's hopes of a finals place already dashed, I gave Melbourne my support. Or maybe I jumped on the bandwagon. The return of their 'favourite son', Ron Barassi, as coach had failed to yield the desired results, just as Jesaulenko was unable to assist the Saints, and now a newcomer to the job, John Northey, was shaping Melbourne into a finals side. I could appreciate their position, and vicariously enjoyed Demon victories as much as somebody emotionally tied to another team is allowed. I soon discovered that whomever I supported, the umpires would go against them.

Melbourne was buoyed by a barnstorming bunch of young blokes, who combined with Flower's return to form, Greg Healy's courageous captaincy and Brian Wilson's weekly weight of possessions to help make them genuine premiership contenders. The Demons beat the Doggies that day. The following week's infamous final, in which Melbourne's Irish import Jim Stynes stepped over the mark to give Hawthorn the game, cut me almost as deeply as if it had been St Kilda in the situation.

The same shadow support surfaced within me a year earlier, as Robert Walls led the Lions to many more wins than they were used to. I was as overjoyed as most Fitzroy followers when he with the thighs like tree trunks, Micky Conlan, kicked a magnificent last-gasp running goal to snatch the elimination final from Essendon by a single point. As thousands of ecstatic supporters celebrated long after the final siren, I studied their mood, soaking in what it felt like to finally enjoy a taste of success after so long.

With Footscray having made the final five the year before that, courtesy of their methodical coach, Micky Malthouse, and the form of recruit Brad Hardie (who won the Brownlow in that, his first League season), I felt alone, left behind. If all the other cellar-dwelling teams were doing it, why couldn't we? Would St Kilda ever make their way out of the mire? My patience was wearing thin. St Kilda's wooden-spoon collection was colossal: bottom of the ladder twenty-two times! While the other sides shuffled positions on the ladder, we seemed to have the anchor down.

The Mad Dog

Standing room at the MCG enabled me to meet Robbie Muir, a footballer famous for his pugilistic abilities. St Kilda seconds were playing Hawthorn in a reserves grand final or something. I say 'or something' to give the impression it wasn't important to me, to try and disguise the fact that seeing the Saints in action in September felt fabulous, seconds side or not.

As I'm waiting for a Hawk-supporting mate of mine, Robbie Muir rolls up, stands next to me and starts watching the game. I introduce myself and carry on about his career, asking him about himself, and it turns out he's also waiting for a friend. 'It's a dry argument', I mention. 'How about a cold can to kill some time?' We speak a little longer and that first beer doesn't touch the sides. Then I realise. It's official. I'm drinking with Robbie Muir. After being told for the first two quarters that it was my shout, I considered suggesting to Robbie that it might be his round some time soon. Then I thought about it again and bought two more beers.

Robbie Muir had gone on the rampage for the final time a few seasons earlier, against Carlton at Princes Park. He'd followed through with an elbow seconds after his opponent, Val Perovic had disposed of the ball downfield. Perovic hit the ground like a sack of spuds. 'Woof!', shouted the Saints supporters. Muir had a marvellous habit of hitting someone, then removing his mouthguard and asking the umpire: 'Did you see that!', implying it was *he* who somehow had been the victim. On this occasion, umpire Kevin Smith paid a downfield free kick and took his book out to report Muir for reckless play. Not that he didn't know his number. Muir's number thirty-two had gained plenty of attention previously from the men in white, and deservedly so, I suppose, but on this occasion 'Mad Dog' Muir went ballistic. Smith, instead of leaving him to unleash a barrage of bad language to no-one in particular, continued to follow Muir, repeatedly confronting him face-to-face, like a persistent encyclopaedia salesman. Muir couldn't walk away without Smith cutting him off, writing down his every word. This infuriated the Mad Dog even further, and to this day I'm surprised Kevin Smith didn't cop a hard right to the head. The ensuing eight-week suspension was ultimately the end of his career.

For a moment there, that match looked like becoming the most violent day in football folklore. As it stands, that honour remains in the hands of John Bourke, the former Collingwood reserves player who flattened an opponent, an umpire and, last but not least, a spectator in the outer during an Army Reserve Cup game. Channel Seven's special-comments man that day, 'Slug' Jordan, made a memorable event even more memorable by contributing the immortal line: 'He's done well, the boy. He's done well'. Fabulous Phil Carman was old news overnight.

CHAPTER TWENTY-THREE

The Wagga Wagga Adventure

In 1989, Simon and I decided, along with a few friends, to see the Saints in Sydney for the first time. Finances and a sense of adventure determined rail would be our mode of transport. It was eight o'clock on a Friday evening when we pulled out of Spencer Street station, bound for New South Wales. The trip takes thirteen hours. By ten past eight the bar may as well have been our own bed, so comfortable had we made ourselves in it. Sitting alongside Simon and me were Shane from Syndal Tech, Steve the Postie, Fonzie and Fats. To quote Bazza McKenzie, we'd developed 'a thirst you could flamin' photograph', and were keen to quench it. Four hours on, as the clock struck twelve, we were tired, emotional and ready for some shut-eye. However, we were maintaining our momentum, and as there was no aggro evident, the barman, who at this point had become 'our bessht mate', made us an offer. The bar was due to close, but if we promised to drink it dry — a feat that apparently had never been achieved — then he was prepared to bend the rules. The gauntlet had been firmly thrown down. The challenge was on.

By two in the morning, the fridges were empty and we were full. Staggering back to our seats, we began asking the other passengers why they were so miserable (as happy people tend to do), when in fact, most of them were asleep. We'd have to continue the party ourselves. While singing *When The Saints Go Marching In*, Steve reached for his bag in the rack above us, searching for some Scotch he'd stashed. The bag came crashing down onto the table between us, smashing the bottle and splashing the Scotch everywhere. At this point the conductor appeared, accusing us of possessing unlicensed liquor. He looked like Ronnie Blaskett, the ventriloquist, which was confusing and made me feel squiffy. 'I don't know what you are talking about', said Steve, crimson-faced and stinking of Johnny Walker. Meanwhile, at the end of the aisle, Fonzie had fallen short in his attempt to be sick in the sink and instead had spewed on someone's shoes. We were treading close to trouble.

Next thing we knew, the train had reached Wagga Wagga station. 'Alright fellas, off! The lot of you', the conductor demanded in the darkness. We tried to explain the situation, but things had reached a stalemate when the argument was interrupted by the sound of approaching sirens. 'Christ! It's the cops', Simon shouted, so we bolted, bags in hand, scattering like students reacting to tear gas at a demonstration.

The scene so far. It's the middle of the night in the middle of nowhere, and six drunks are running in all directions, ordered off a Sydney-bound express, with the flashing blue lights of the law in pursuit. In the background, we could hear the sound of our train rumbling away along the tracks. I'd managed to find two factories built back-to-back, with just enough space to squeeze myself in between. I stood there, still and silent, my mind muddled with alcohol, unable to comprehend exactly what was going on. Everything had happened so fast. I don't imagine they tried too hard to find us, and eventually, the cops headed back to headquarters, leaving us to locate each other in soft whispers through the shadows.

Immediately after the event, a fight seemed certain, but it never eventuated. Instead, we attempted to put the pieces together, laying the blame at each other's feet. What's more, where the hell was Wagga Wagga? The whys, the wherefores and the hows of our swift departure from that train are debated to this day. Tempers flared. We were stranded, equally distant from both our Melbourne homes and our Sydney destination, the SCG. What to do? The decision was unanimous. We'd come this far, we agreed, so we'd follow the original plan, even if it broke our budget. Six blokes hitch-hiking proved spectacularly unsuccessful. Passing trucks merely tooted their horns in contempt. The bus depot, we discovered, had been warned about us in advance, but luckily, the incoming driver decided to take pity on us. And so we arrived at the Sydney Cricket Ground.

We hoped to harass the infamous white-haired pensioner Swans supporters who sat behind the goals, waving wildly, as seen on telly every second Sunday, but were unable to enter their area. We stood on The Hill, but it was poorly populated and didn't seem recognisable to us as the lively place we'd seen on telly during summer cricket matches. Still, at least the result was familiar — the Saints received a thrashing. Warwick Capper kicked six goals and used Saint full back Danny Frawley as a stepladder all afternoon. The scoreboard, in particular, got on our goat, blasting out the same ridiculous song of celebration after every goal from the home side. We amused ourselves by singing our own variations. Somehow, we managed to make it back to Melbourne without further major incident.

The Triumphant Return

My failure as a footballer was due to a serious skill shortage under pressure. I was unable to initiate any piece of play. An average training session saw me matching my team-mates in most skills. My limitations arose only under match conditions — in other words, when it mattered. Kicking out from goal, taking a mark or accepting a free kick provided no problem, as all these situations allowed me a few seconds to assess the state of play. Gaining possession with the ball bouncing free was when I became confused. The pressure in such situations was too intense for my mind to master. The action always left me behind. The pack would split in several directions, leaving me standing still.

Whereas Greg 'Diesel' Williams' perfect peripheral vision seemed to give him extra time, with other players seemingly 'freeze-framed' while the ball was in his hands, I felt as if the other players were in fast-forward while I was on pause. I couldn't even do a decent bushman's blow. When I held one nostril shut and tried to express the excess snot, it always ended up clinging to my face and running along my arm instead of heading towards the ground.

The former Port Melbourne and Footscray full forward Fred Cook, over six feet in height and ruggedly handsome, turned up to training one night with a view to playing for our senior side. Club officials were over the moon. I was paired with him during the drills, and at the age of forty-four, the infamous ex-junkie still took one-handed marks on the run in the pouring rain. Despite the fact that his belly overhung and his head looked hung-over, I'd never seen such skills.

Training rarely varied at any club. The poorly lit oval echoed with a dozen different nicknames, yelled repeatedly as handballs were called for during drills. 'Macca, Macca, Macca, Macca, Macca!'

Fred Cook wasn't seen again after that first training session, but I was delighted to learn that even *he* does push-ups with an eye on the coach, sitting a few out when he's out of view. It was an old trick of mine. Rest on palms and knees, but keep counting out loud, as if you're doing 'em anyway. 'Seventeen, puff, eighteen, puff, nineteen ...'

Oakleigh Districts Football Club represented my final fling at football glory. The South-East Suburban League contains some of the toughest teams in the country. Oakleigh Districts produced David Rhys-Jones, who early in his career was one of the most notoriously vigorous players the game had seen. I hadn't played since the Under 16s. Six feet three, yet just eleven stone, I could've hidden behind the goal post. Senior footy meant a serious mouthguard. This time I needed more than an over-the-counter creation. The dentist's appointment involved biting into a rubber dish full of some gummy pink fluorescent fluid that tasted like cough medicine. When the finished product arrived a week later, it fitted so snugly that I wore the marvellous bright-white mouthguard around the house for the sheer pleasure of it.

Five minutes into the third quarter, my big moment arrived. Off came the dressing gown and I was limbering up, doing some good old-fashioned jogging on the spot. Then, high-fiving the player I was replacing, away I went. Coming on against Mount Waverley on their home ground, with my extra-long laces wrapped around and under my boots about twelve bloody times, I was more than a little nervous, wondering if I really could cut it in an adult competition.

Picking up the in-form full forward, I instantly adopted the Mick Gayfer method: I held onto his jumper. The former Collingwood defender had been criticised in the press by Dermot Brereton, who claimed his negative tactics were against the rules and used to disguise a lack of ability. I can't speak on Gayfer's behalf, but Brereton's description was an accurate summary of my reason for illegally holding on to *my* opponents. It was a sure-fire way of winning the contest. In this case, it was crucial. I was determined that my first outing was *not* going to end in humiliating failure. My team-mates had a willing reputation, so I figured that if the fists flew, all I'd have to do was avoid the first few and wait for the cavalry to arrive.

Mount Waverley's winger came steaming out of the centre. My opponent, having kicked five so far on our usual full back, attempted a lead, but his timing was hampered by my subtle scragging. I'd ruined his rhythm. As he ran too far under the ball, I stayed behind and marked by myself. 'Try that again and I'll punch you in the fuckin' face', he warned. He wasn't very big, but his confidence made me uncomfortable. 'I'm shaking in my boots, mate', I replied, the sarcastic tone belying my genuine fear.

Minutes later. Same winger, same lead, same tactic. This time, the full forward punched me in the fuckin' face. He was a man of his word. I punched him back. We wrestled each other to the ground, still trading blows. Luckily, just in time, in came a cavalcade of opposing colours. It was not a pretty sight. Our blokes revelled in the rough stuff and, after some initial strong resistance, soon gained supremacy. The sound of knuckle on jaw is always sickening, even as a one-off, let alone when there are so many that it sounds like a herd of horses galloping down a road. As we resumed our positions, I was a bit shaken, but he was a ghost of his former self. When the final siren sounded, he hadn't kicked a goal on me. We lost, after a commendable comeback, but the coach liked what he saw. I'd hardly had a touch, but at least I'd stopped the rot, and thereafter found a regular role at full back.

After six similar efforts, I felt satisfied for the first time in my footballing life. We were winning, my kick-outs from goal tended to go to someone on our side, and opposition full forwards were scoring fuck all. At training, team-mates jokingly called me 'the giant killer'. The captain of the firsts took such a shine to me that he sneakily smeared a thin film of Deep Heat in my spare pair of undies, a touching male-bonding gesture.

Post-match piss-ups began to take on extra importance. 'We can drink, We can fight, We can fuck all bloody night, We are the boys from Oak-er-leigh.' As I write these lines, I have some understanding of why we were so frustrated in the girlfriend department. Following a string of failed attempts at attracting the opposite sex, most blokes I knew found bare-faced lies their best remaining option. Pretending to be a League footballer was a favourite fib, if only because previously uninterested girls usually did an about-face on being told of their suitor's skills with a Sherrin. 'Reserves at the moment. Not far off a senior game' was the standard cover, just in case they knew their stuff or checked with a friend who did. (However, I once made a sexual conquest by finally admitting, after two hours of furious denial, that I was, in fact, the drummer from the Rockmelons.)

Favouring the Forrester's Arms in Oakleigh, the closest bar presenting live bands, we sang along with a string of cover bands from Scat to Captain Spalding, all of whom played the same songs, with *Khe Sahn* as the encore every time. Nicabellas was another of our haunts, and even the Tunnel took our fancy a few times. First choice of footy stars, the Tunnel went off at weekends.

Whenever a woman was able to ignore our boorish behaviour and make one of us aware of her initial interest, the other blokes pulled a prank known as 'The Snake', quickly extinguishing any flames our friend may have fanned. Waiting until the man with a chance had done his groundwork and gone for a wee, someone would seize the opportunity to lie to the woman about what a villain her potential partner was. False yarns were woven until she took one to be true. Alimony, alcoholism, infidelity, anything. It always worked. By the time the bloke returned, the lady had vanished. The perpetrator of a successful Snake was held in high regard — even, eventually, reluctantly, by the victim himself.

Anyone falling behind the beer-drinking pace on these evenings out was frowned upon. My sure-fire method of escape involved playing 'The Phantom, ghost who walks'. The rules? Pretend you're off to buy a few pots, then secretly shuffle outside and into a cab. If this is done well, and correctly timed, the mates you left behind won't even notice your absence until your head has hit the pillow at home.

Deep down I dreamt of getting a game in Oakleigh District's senior side. If that happened, maybe a talent scout would see me play well. Then, if I could put on some weight, who knows? Who knows?! Everybody knew. Even me. I was cheating. Within his limitations, the skinny bloke was having a purple patch. I wasn't expected to last two weeks. It doesn't take much for delusions of grandeur to take hold. If I had a less than one per cent chance of improving to the point where I played senior footy, it was a better chance than I'd had two months before. Enough for me to let my imagination run wild. I thought of previous players who'd been plucked from obscurity: Collingwood's Ian McMullen from the Amateurs, Melbourne's Jim Stynes from Ireland, Paul Meldrum, who walked in off the street and asked if he could train with Carlton, then became a premiership player. I wrote narcissistic headlines in my head. For a brief period of time, I was ten again.

To possess the basic skills yet be unable to expand upon them was perhaps more frustrating than lacking the basic skills in the first place. Was Phillip Franklynstein of the Nottinghill Bs aware of his utter hopelessness? If so, did he know he was destined to remain that way for the term of his footballing life? Surely such knowledge, despite its inherent heartache, would have helped him sleep easier. Or was he, like me, cursed by an eternal optimism? Did he believe that once the gawky years of adolescence were behind him, everything would fall into place? If not, then why did he persist in playing? Perhaps because if the truth hurts, then it's easier to avoid it a little longer. Fate will make you face the facts eventually, but we clung to our dream until it was run over by reality.

The Iron Fist

My football career was over as soon as it began, but not before I threw the perfect punch. We were a fair way in front against East Brighton when our ruckman went off injured. I was told to contest the centre bounces — an appealing idea in front of our home crowd. I was going okay, and it meant a lot to get a kick in front of the senior players as they gradually arrived for the main game.

Following a boundary throw-in, I felt a whoosh of air rush through my hair. I turned, to see our rover racing towards my immediate opponent, anger in his eyes. The other team's ruckman, six feet six, seventeen stone and aged about thirty-three, was worried I might give him the runaround and had tried to king-hit me from behind. I joined our rover in remonstrating with the ruckman. He couldn't even connect when I was stationary and facing the other way. What's more, he'd stolen Merv Hughes' moustache. The scuffle ceased and I forgot the whole thing.

Leaping as part of a pack some ten minutes later, I felt a blind blow to the jaw like I'd been hit with a brick. It felt as if I'd swallowed my tongue. My knees buckled. The lights went out. Picking myself up, a quick check suggested no broken bones but enough pain to panic. Fear turned to fury when I realised who had done the damage. He was fifteen feet away on the flank. I stormed towards him, screaming abuse. 'What are ya gonna do about it?' he goaded me, unconcerned in view of our comparative size and beckoning me to keep on coming. In my mood, it was easy to oblige.

Suddenly, he was on his back in front of me. Blood poured from his face, turning the white of his jumper red. Car horns honked. An all-in brawl broke out around me. I wandered away in a daze, eyes spinning like tops. The runner rushed me off the ground. I'd landed a straight left square on his snout before either of us knew it was coming. He dropped like a factory chimney exploding inwards. Everything went silent for a few seconds. Then the dust settled, the sound returned and it all went off.

I've since wondered about murderers who claim to have no memory of the fatal event. I know I wanted to hurt him. I know he was hurt. I recall the approach and the retreat, but the point of contact is a blank. If my decision had been a conscious one, I'd have elected to use my right hand, my natural side. It was a strange sensation. Seconds after I'd snotted him, the adrenaline rush was unbelievable, even better than streaking. After the game, he wanted to be my mate! I still had the shakes. I didn't want to know.

He'd got up during the full-on fighting, swung a random round-arm towards one of our wingers, and was reported. Not long after tribunal night, the ongoing pain made me realise I must've busted a bone in my left hand. I was going to be out for the last few weeks of the season, so I decided to go out on top and retire on the spot. Nobody noticed.

The next morning, I woke to a shocking realisation. I was never going to play for St Kilda. The idea had probably never crossed anyone's mind but mine anyway, even though I *had* cut my name out of the *Waverley Gazette* Nottinghill B-team report on those rare occasions I was mentioned, secretly sending it to St Kilda's recruiting officer. Looking back, I wondered why it had taken me this long to work it out! Even Robert Harvey playing his first senior game, aged sixteen, watched by me, aged nineteen, had not been enough of a hint. Life was just a little bit greyer from that moment on.

CHAPTER TWENTY-FOUR

The Wedding

It was at Derbys Nitespot that I assisted Mark in getting married. Three years earlier, not long after I'd met Shaggy's sister, a woman approached me at the bar. I thought my ship had come in again, but was quickly put in my place when she asked me where my brother was. She handed me her phone number, demanding I pass it on to Mark, who apparently had failed to ring her as arranged. I did as she asked, and the rest is history. Mark and Andrea were married. Unfortunately for Simon and me, St Kilda also chose to make history on that day.

Yes, they tied the knot on a Saturday afternoon during the footy season! Missing a game was bad enough, but the Saints' win against Hawthorn that day was their first over the Hawks in the whole time we'd been following football. While we watched the newlyweds signing the wedding book to the strains of a lady singing *The First Time Ever I Saw Your Face*, Simon and I strained to hear our tiny, tinny tranny for details of the three-point thriller at Moorabbin. After so many years of loyalty to both Mark and the Saints, we didn't deserve such treatment.

Social Status

In Melbourne, the footy side you support has long been considered a good indication of both your personality and your social status. I like to think it was no coincidence that as a Saints supporter, my first car was a 1960s Holden, whereas one of my Collingwood-supporting mates drove a 1970s Monaro. If I were to take the first-car analogy a step further, the Essendon supporters I knew had usually lost their licence, whereas those who favoured Fitzroy couldn't afford a car in the first place.

As Mecca is to Muslims, so each club's home ground is its supporters' centre of worship. Moorabbin was the axis of St Kilda's ideology. Never has a football club's motto so appropriately described what was asked of its followers — and rarely have a football club's followers adhered so strictly to it: 'Fortius Quo Fidelius' (Strength Through Loyalty). In other words, 'We Will Continue To Turn Up Despite Being Repeatedly Trounced'. Perhaps 'Success Through Loyalty' would have been preferable, but as Mum often said in answer to my complaints about the vegetables she'd served up: 'You get what you're given in this world'.

As it was, 'Strength Through Loyalty' suggested we were *above* winning. If your child was not succeeding at school, would you ditch it and adopt another? Of course not. It was not even a consideration. Once we had made our choice, it was forever. We just had to wear it. I couldn't define the personality or social status of the average St Kilda supporter, but I could explain what it *wasn't*. There were no obvious signs of wealth or poverty. On our feet were Blundstone boots and adidas runners. We were probably watchers of *Seven Nightly News*, seeing Nine as silk and Ten as sandpaper. Factually, morally and metaphorically, our fabric would be suede. We were inner suburban. We might not have done a degree in Literature, but we'd read books other than biographies by Chopper Read. Career options veered somewhere between tradesmen and creative types. In fact, to describe our team as creative tradesmen wouldn't have been far off the mark, so an alliance was evident.

Adelaide Alive

In 1991, Adelaide was launched as the AFL's newest club. With teams now based in Adelaide, Brisbane, Perth and Sydney, the national vision had been realised. The Crows made an impact by thrashing Hawthorn on debut, but couldn't sustain that standard through their first season. They still produced some fine performances, unveiling a talented team including Nigel Smart, Andrew Jarman and ruckman Shaun Rehn.

Having learnt our lesson about interstate train travel, we arrived by plane on the Friday night, intending to watch the game before running amok around Adelaide. The Saints were on the verge of making the finals and

Plugger was seeking seven goals to make his season's total a nice, round one hundred. Simon and I were joined on this occasion by John Kerry, a former Syndal Tech schoolmate. Of restricted height, yet noted for his bone-crunching shirt-fronts, Johnny was a Richmond supporter with an eye for action. He sniffed trouble like a bloodhound.

Hindley Street was where it all happened. In the heart of Adelaide, it contained a large number of all night bars, clubs and strip joints. Selecting the cheapest digs on the main drag, we adjourned to our rooms for some pre-game grooming. We were soon consulting each other for ideas on the origins of various smells, stains and scorch marks on our allotted bedding. The place was a disgrace (with carpets so cheap, the static build-up shot lightning bolts through my body whenever I touched something metal), but considering the manager at the downstairs desk bore an unnerving resemblance to Norman Bates from the 'Psycho' films, we decided it didn't warrant a complaint.

By all reports, and from the evidence we'd seen on the small screen, the pro-Crow crowd was a lynch mob. Safe inside a taxi, we took advantage of the traffic jam to jeer any Adelaide supporters we saw along the way. Football Park was packed to capacity to watch the Saints reign supreme. Plugger put on a spectacular show, notching up the ton in quick time, though with so few Saints supporters and so many security men, we didn't make it onto the ground, much to our disgust. For the first time in my memory, the St Kilda players went out of their way to applaud their own supporters following the final siren. The show of appreciation made us feel special. We entered the ground expecting a punch-up, but found the Adelaide audience a pleasant surprise.

After the match, we hit the city like a cyclone. First stop: the Adelaide Casino. Victoria had yet to legalise gambling, so this was like visiting Las Vegas. I was transfixed by the two-up table, particularly the punters who offered the coins verbal encouragement, as if they were alive and able to respond accordingly. It was at a nightclub somewhere in Glenelg that there was a curious commotion at the door and in walked the famous West Indian fast bowler, all six feet eight of him, Joel Garner, accompanied by the legendary Dennis Lillee. Blokes were doing double-takes in disbelief. All around the bar, women lost interest in anyone they were speaking with. All-time cricketing kings, the West Indian players had star quality by the bucketload. None of this unassuming sportsman stuff; it was obvious they were out for a good time, in town for a fund-raising function to honour South Australian cricketer David Hookes in his Testimonial Year. So began a pub crawl I will never forget.

Lillee and Garner attracted an immediate following, mixing easily among the crowd, and encouraged us to come along, reaching each new pub with an ever-expanding party. Sportsmen must endure post-game groupies and parasites all over the place, but these two seemed to be actually enjoying the attention, although it's possible that they just didn't have the time to punch us *all*. In either case, Dennis Lillee was the perfect gentleman as I explained how he'd helped beat boredom during Maths at primary school. See, the number 337717 spells 'LILLEE' on a calculator screen if you turn it upside down, a fact which provided me with hours of fun. As the only other possible words were BOOBS (58008), HELLO (07734), and SHELL OIL (710 77345), he was easily the most interesting option. Unlike myself in the bar at that moment.

Self-Belief

Years before at Pinewood Primary, 'Show and Tell' had quickly become my favourite class. Here was a chance to boast openly about your best and most interesting possessions. This brilliantly disguised method of promoting social and speaking skills saw a succession of Tonka trucks, yo-yos and Barbie dolls presented to an enraptured audience. Each day a new child, in alphabetical order, was given an opportunity to make their classmates envious. The trick was to bring something expensive, brand new, or both. One morning, a girl got up who looked scruffy, though not actually dirty or unwashed, and who had long, strawberry-blonde hair and a flowing, old-fashioned floral frock. We were intrigued before she even began. Then, from behind her back, she produced the cylindrical, cardboard core of a toilet roll. We were stunned. Miss Baylam half-stood in her seat, as if to prevent the girl guaranteeing herself a lifetime of ridicule, but the girl began to speak with such rapidly increasing confidence that the teacher sat back, mouth agape.

'Today I have brought for show and tell, THIS! I don't know what it is called, but it can be lots of things'. Placing it on the teacher's desk and pressing her open palms on top, she explained, 'It can be a rolling pin'. She then put it to her mouth and made a noise. 'It can be a trumpet', before holding it up to her eye, 'and it can be a telescope'.

At this point, we burst into a rapturous ovation. Miss Baylam retrieved a tissue from up her sleeve and wiped away a tear. When I first saw what the girl had in her hand, I almost laughed out loud. Then I thought about shouting something insulting. Then I felt so sad for her that my stomach ached. From the moment she spoke, however, she was so compelling, so enthusiastic, so full of self-belief, that I think I fell in love — with her, with life, with the idea of making something from nothing. Previously unfelt emotions swirled around inside me until I felt seasick. The girl took her seat, the class continued and I spent the rest of the day wondering if she'd swap her toilet roll for my 'Six Million Dollar Man' doll.

As St Kilda's odds of reaching the finals improved, we noticed a new spring in their step, even a sparkle in their eyes. For the first time since we'd been following the Saints, they seemed to go into games as if they *would* win.

Their new approach gave us genuine hope. If St Kilda's players and supporters could believe in the team for a little longer, believe in themselves, like that little girl at Pinewood Primary, if they could experience a similar unquestionable self-confidence, if they told themselves they were going to win, then who was to say they couldn't?

CHAPTER TWENTY-FIVE

The Final Siren

It was official, we were in the finals, finally. We danced in the outer with anyone willing. Strangers hugged each other happily, crying tears of triumph. The players piled on top of each other in front of the members, a writhing orgy of arms and legs clad in red, white and black. Grandmas waved their scarves in the stands, the capacity crowd moved as one.

Simon and I screamed in each others faces, each spouting one endless stream of nonsensical joy.

'YOUFUCKENBEAUTY, WE'VEFUCKENDUNNITT, YEEEAAAAHHHHH!!!!!!!!!!!!!!!!!!!!!'

The victory over Adelaide in Round Twenty-Two of the twenty-four-round season inched St Kilda closer to what Simon and I had dreamed of since we first saw the word 'Fuck' written on the warehouse wall at Moorabbin. The following week, the Saints gave the Brisbane Bears an old-fashioned mauling. We won by exactly twenty goals in a game where Plugger produced the best running goal I've ever seen and Russell Morris pulled in twenty-two marks at centre half-back. (We called Russell Morris 'Hector', after the road-safety cat. They shared similar theories. When Morris gained possession, he suffered from overwhelming indecision, so he'd stop at the kerb, look to the right, look to the left and look to the right again.) It was a display of unadulterated domination. After four quarters of football finer than anything my imagination could have concocted.

Then came the theme song. At full volume. Fifty times in a row. All the previous pain was worth it. Every humiliating hiding at Hawthorn's hands, each easy win by Essendon, countless crushing defeats courtesy of Carlton — they all helped put this moment almost beyond belief. It was the happiest day I'd known. This was what I'd wanted through my childhood, my adolescence, my manhood. We were gonna see St Kilda's senior side compete in September!

The following week's win over Sydney was an enjoyable diversion, the Saints sending the Swans packing in the final game of the home-and-away season. It was only a year since we'd survived the unexpected stop in Wagga Wagga on our way to watching Warwick Capper and his comrades kick our arse all over the SCG.

Adelaide's addition to the League had seen the VFL officially renamed the AFL. It also created an uneven number of teams, so the Final Five became a Final Six. The complications of the system prompted endless hours of expert argument. Suffice it to say that, in the end, the Saints were to play Geelong, who had finished third, in an elimination final. One loss and it would all be over. In any previous season, finishing third would've earned a double chance at finals time. In this instance, however, teams finishing third and fourth gained nothing over those finishing fifth and sixth. It was a system that was quickly abolished.

That week was like living in Utopia. Thousands turned up to training. Supporters of other sides chose the Saints as their finals team and newspapers were selling on the back of stories about St Kilda, but it wasn't until Eddie McGuire arrived with a camera crew that I knew we'd smashed through to the big time. The glaring media spotlight was a novelty for us and we bathed in the attention. Friends congratulated Simon and I as if we represented the Saints ourselves. I suppose we did in a way. To them, as always, we represented the struggle St Kilda's players and supporters had suffered for far too long. Now the wait was over.

At Waverley Park on the Friday night before the big game, the various groups who'd gathered behind the goals at Moorabbin during the bad times joined forces once again in the carpark, faces painted, for an all-night finals fiesta. While we wanted our side to win more than anything else on earth, experience suggested we make the most of this opportunity, for who knew when we'd have the chance again? Male-bonding rituals were rife throughout the wee hours. Such was the mood that when a few girls showed up, we weren't even uncomfortable. The sniff of success relaxed our sexist standards. As the surrounding suburbs enjoyed their slumber, our world was a boisterous bonanza of footy ballads, cold beer and bonfires, encircled by a shabby collection of second-hand cars and folding chairs. As the sun came up, we tucked into a chicken and champagne breakfast. This was living.

So Close . . .

Elimination final day, 1991. The unbearable anticipation ends as St Kilda burst through the banner, the side at full strength. *Football Record* in hand, we tick the players off as the tight-knit group run laps around the centre square. 'Hang on a minute, who's that out there?' we hear someone shout. The Saints have opened the batting with Craig McDermott, by including Ricky Nixon at the last minute. The frizzy-haired ex-Carlton defender had been brought in, unannounced, to assist the likes of Danny Frawley and Russell Morris in containing champion Geelong forwards Ablett and Brownless. Geelong's defence face their own problems in Lockett and Loewe, but have stuck to their selected side.

The game is played at a blistering pace. Hocking controls the centre for the Cats. Harvey keeps the Saints blazing forward. At half-time, we have a three-goal lead and are sitting pretty. By three-quarter time, though, things have taken a distinct turn for the worse, with Geelong now one point in front. Frawley has limped off with a bad leg, while Ablett's steamrolled both David Grant and Nathan Burke right out of the game. In our favour, Winmar's running riot. Lazar Vidovic and Brett Bowey are doing a sterling job, rucking and roving respectively. At opposite ends, Plugger and Billy Brownless are on fire. The final quarter is furious. The Saints play gallantly, brilliantly, but at the final siren, the Cats are seven points in front.

The Rise

The following year, the Saints again performed to their peak, providing many fine memories (including a superb one-point win over Collingwood in front of 80,000 at the MCG), but the year is notable for the fact that Moorabbin ceased to be. Various reasons were offered up by St Kilda and the AFL for our move to Waverley Park as co-tenants with Hawthorn. In Round Twenty, St Kilda defeated Fitzroy by eighteen points at Moorabin and I bid a fond farewell to my favourite place on earth. I have photos of us all, wearing 'I Was There For The Last Bounce At Moorabbin' badges and looking grief-stricken. It was a great loss.

When your hopes and dreams have been lived out on a certain piece of land, the emotional wrench when it disappears reflects the fact that part of your personal history disappears with it. Not long afterwards, Syndal Tech, my secondary school, was demolished. In a matter of months, my entire life history had been erased. As Simon and I, drunk and depressed, stumbled down Linton Street, never to watch a senior game at Moorabbin again, we stopped to look at the word on the wall one final time. 'Fuck'. It seemed to sum things up rather well.

We went on to see our beloved Saints beat Collingwood in the second elimination final, pushing ourselves even closer to The Big One. What pure pleasure! Even better, one of the behind-the-goals-at-Moorabbin blokes (who repositioned themselves, as a unit, in Bay Thirty-Six, standing on the outer wing at Waverley Park) arranged a raffle around Plugger's tally at game's end. From a range of zero goals, zero behinds to fifteen goals, ten behinds, I plucked out eight goals, two behinds. Thank you! At the game's end, I had two hundred bucks in my back pocket, fifty going on the bar and the rest towards my forthcoming flight to England. I'd decided to place a long-odds bet — on making something of myself overseas. Perhaps I was looking for a way to replace what had been taken away. The flight had been booked to depart four days after the grand final, which I'd been hoping we might win. But we lost to Footscray in the first semi-final and the season was over.

CHAPTER TWENTY-SIX

The Fall

I am unable to comment on the following four seasons, as I was overseas for much of this time, able to return for just three months, during the summer of 1995/96. This is what I know to have taken place.

1993: St Kilda slips to twelfth. Stab me.

1994: Stan Alves takes over as coach from the sacked Ken Sheldon. St Kilda slips to thirteenth. Shoot me.

1995: Lockett leaves St Kilda, then kicks one hundred and ten goals in his first season for Sydney. St Kilda slips to fourteenth. Slice me into little shreds.

The 1996 season got off to a spectacular start when St Kilda beat Carlton to win the Ansett Cup grand final. Stuck overseas, I could not blow so much dough on a flight for a pre-season competition, especially as I'd flown back to London two months earlier, having chosen, after much consideration, the Boxing Day Test over the Ansett Cup as the sporting focus of my holiday. I thought I'd be able to handle it *if* the Saints went on to win such an event in my absence. I was wrong. Drunken phone calls from Sim, Steve the Postie, Shane from Syndal Tech and Young

Jason (not to mention Fats, now a seasoned Sainter following his defection from the Swans after their Sydney move) served to make me resent St Kilda for months. St Kilda finished the home-and-away season in tenth position, which would've seemed almost satisfying if that Ansett Cup win hadn't got our hopes up.

CHAPTER TWENTY-SEVEN

Mr High-In-The-Sky

It was not yet dark when I returned to my London flat on the evening of 26 April 1996. Easing the front door open, I saw the red light flashing on my answer-machine, indicating someone had left me a message — not an unusual occurrence, so I set my keys on the coffee table and went for a wee before sitting down with a notepad and pressing 'Play'.

Mum's voice sounded sombre and I immediately feared the worst. I felt reassured when she said: 'Now, *we're* all okay', and heard myself exhale with relief. She continued: 'But there's some sad news I thought you'd want to hear. Trevor Barker died in his sleep last night'. She said other things, but I didn't hear them. Indigestion seemed to attack me on the spot. It crept slowly up my throat, where it formed a lump. It hurt in there, that lump. I swallowed, in the hope it would go away, but it didn't. A strange sensation rose from my toes to my nose, repeatedly, like a series of hot flushes, the space between them reducing rapidly. My bottom lip began to fold back on itself outwardly and my eyes closed themselves with pressure and permanence, as if I was an Olympic weight-lifter straining to hold the sagging bar above my head until the buzzer goes. I tried to stop, but it was no use. This emotion was so overpowering, I conceded defeat and chose to go with the flow. I'd cried before, as a boy and as a man. Love, hate, fear, frustration, pleasure, pain — all had activated my tear ducts at one time or other. But this was something else altogether. I felt like an infant animal left behind by its family, unable to cope alone in the wilderness. Then and there, as I struggled to digest Mum's message, the death of Trevor Barker represented not only the loss of his life, but also a loss of innocence, a loss of whatever impressionable part of me had been so affected by his face on the footy card all those years ago. Growing up in Glen Waverley, with no signs of imminent war, depression or economic collapse, we were free to dream. Lucky people in a lucky country. Trevor Barker had long blond hair. Trevor Barker played for St Kilda. Trevor Barker took screamers and kicked miraculous goals. Trevor Barker was always surrounded by gorgeous girls. Trevor Barker was an angel, a god. I dreamed of doing these things, and saw no reason why *he* shouldn't one day be *me*. The answer-machine message was a lengthy one, and by the time I'd stopped bawling, Mum had started. There we were, mother and son, at opposite ends of the earth, distraught over the death of a sports star we didn't know.

Footy Fate

I think Mum knew something of what Trevor Barker meant to me — maybe in more depth than I did. Barker gave me a purpose, an aim, something on which to set my sights. I never came close to emulating his achievements on the footy field, but my drive to succeed, the need to make something of myself, started when I saw that footy card. I simply had to redirect my energy upon realising that the Saints, screamers and sex sirens were well beyond me. When I realised I wouldn't be like Trevor Barker, I didn't put my drive to strive back into the drawer. Missing out on the *main* thing didn't mean spitting the dummy and giving up on *everything*.

What path might my life have taken had I not bought that packet of footy cards? What if I'd been dealt a different hand? After much soul-searching, I concluded that it has all been fate. It had to happen, sooner or later. I was a pawn to my environment: a primary school kid, living in Melbourne suburbia during the 1970s. Everyone else was doing it, so what choice did I have, really? 'If your mates jumped off a cliff, does that mean you would too?' my Mum used to ask if ever I blamed my actions on the fact that others had done the same before me. It was obvious to us both that I *would* jump off that hypothetical cliff if ever it actually materialised. The concept of peer pressure conjures negative images, but my succumbing to peer pressure was a passive, positive reaction. I enjoyed following the crowd.

I wondered what might have happened had Trevor Barker's picture not been in that set of cards. Would Rex Hunt, the only other St Kilda player in that packet, have become my life-long obsession? Somehow, I doubt it. In

Trevor Barker, it was immediately obvious that here was an attractive man. Here was a ladies' man. Here was a man on top of the pack.

If his blond, Hollywood-style attributes were what caught my eye, then what if Hawthorn's Peter Knights' or Essendon's Paul Van Der Haar's had been the first face I saw? Surely, in that case, I'd have been entranced by them instead, and either way I'd have been following a team destined for greatness. No, the fact that Knights and Van Der Haar were exciting, blond high-flyers wouldn't have come into the equation. It was Barker's face on that footy card that had me hypnotised. There was *something* there. If Trevor Barker had played for some other side, the Matchbox car 'Saint' connection could have and would have been ignored.

If he hadn't been in that packet of footy cards, I'd have discovered him some other way.

The Reversal of Fortune

By April 1997, I had been living in London for exactly four and a half years. I had remained a paid-up Saints member, with weekly footy updates delivered by my brother by phone, and felt a good degree of delight or dejection depending on the results. Therefore, after a hideous hiding in Brisbane completed three straight losses at the start of the new season, I phoned the club from London to demand Stan Alves' departure. Rumours of various mergers came and went almost monthly. Some clubs were inevitably going to sink without trace. Times were turbulent and action had to be taken. Alves had been given a good shot and had failed. The steam train of extinction was rocketing around the bend and I felt it was someone else's turn to try and untie us from the tracks.

Then, almost overnight, things turned around. Alves offered his resignation to the senior team at a hastily called crisis meeting. They refused it, wishing to share the blame equally. They analysed their errors as a unit. They started afresh. With the administration showing admirable faith in one and all (thankfully, my phone call fell on deaf ears), the St Kilda Football Club instigated what would become one of the most unlikely and exciting turnarounds since Collingwood rose from 1976 wooden spooners to finish on top of the ladder in 1977. On a tidal wave of emotion, we surfed straight into our first grand final for twenty-six years.

Grand Final Flight

'No-one's kicked a goal since you last rang. There's ten minutes to go. I'll ring you as soon as the final siren sounds. Don't panic.'

On Friday night, 19 September 1997, St Kilda played North Melbourne at the MCG for the right to play in The Big One. Simon's wife, Lisa, was not becoming impatient, but simply had no further news for me. I'd been phoning Melbourne from London every ten minutes throughout the match. Australia is eleven hours ahead of England, which meant it was shortly before midday on a Friday morning in London as the game went into time-on with only a couple of goals in it. 'Don't panic', she says!

'I know, Matthew, I know. I just rang my mum and said, "Listen, I understand no-one's scored since we last spoke, but how is it *looking*? Who's got the momentum? Why doesn't somebody kill Wayne Carey?! I don't care if we have to sacrifice Barry Hall or some other silly bastard, just get us into the grand fucking final"'.

I met Greg Swedosh at Arundel, in the South East area of England. I couldn't work him out. A deep-olive complexion, thick dark hair sitting high on his head, *and* freckles, the type of freckles a red-head has. Little eyes, large smile. Effeminate and macho by turns. Shy, yet prone to shouting. Whatever, he was instantly likeable and he wore the red, white and black. Arundel is where the Australian cricket team traditionally play the opening game of each Ashes tour, against a side selected by the Duke of Norfolk. The ground is one of the most glorious you could ever set eyes on, the perfect environment for our Test players to lose their jet lag. There were a large number of Aussie tourists around the boundary this particular day, yet it was still an unlikely environment to see someone wearing a St Kilda jumper. We both assumed our attire would be unique in such a scenario. As it was, we were like a pair of the same species on Noah's Ark. We'd both been overseas for a couple of years, and tried to out-do each other with the intricacies of our footy memories.

'Remember that bloke from Frankston? Mean face, like a Mafia man. Played about four games on the half-back flank in 1984/85? Might've worn number thirty-six.' It was not really an agreed competition, but we were competing all the same. Greg and I kept in contact, phoning each other if we wanted a dose of footy discussion when it happened to be five in the morning Australian time and we couldn't ring home for it.

While St Kilda battled it out against North Melbourne, there we were, more than ten thousand miles and twenty-four hours away from our friends and family at the MCG, waiting in our respective flats to see whether we needed to catch the first flight home. We were both working, and were therefore unable to take time off on the spot without a very good reason. So, with the costs involved, we had to wait for confirmation of a grand final berth before booking. There was never a question of not going if the Saints made it through. It was painful enough to be absent from the games leading up to this point — *not* just the previous finals, but the storming season that had seen us finish on top of the ladder at the end of the home-and-away season.

The phone rang. I knew it was Lisa. In my state of mind, it sounded more like an alarm going off than a phone ringing. I wanted to ignore it as much as I wanted to answer it. Adopting the rip-the-band-aid-off-rapidly ploy, I didn't so much pick up the phone as *yank* it up to my ear, in the manner Dad reserved for pulling the starter cord on the lawnmower. Lisa was unintelligible, but in the background, I could hear the St Kilda theme song playing on the radio, its static echo pouring from the MCG's public-address system to the other side of the world, via the radio on my brother's kitchen bench. Lisa and I gabbled a bit about Simon being at the game and how he'd be thinking of me now, and I hung up. I had some organising to do. Before that, though, I shed a sparkling tear of undiluted delight.

Flight booked. Work cancelled. Qantas was to carry Greg and me home for what might be the highlight of our lives. Simon, Fats and Young Jason, among other members of the original Moorabbin mob, arranged rostered shifts in the all-night queue for tickets to get us seats. Upon touching down at Tullamarine on the Wednesday, three days before The Big One, Greg and I were met by family and went our separate ways, agreeing to celebrate our victory on the return trip.

Grand Final Eve

We weren't in much of a drinking mood when we met up at Young & Jackson's before the grand final parade. Chloe had been moved upstairs for security reasons but we didn't bother going up to give our regards. The parade came and went without incident, or suprisingly, excitement. With the afternoon free, Simon, Fats, young Jason and I hit on the idea of heading to the MCG. With all the bustle of the pre-game preparations, we expected to stroll through a tradesman's entrance and into the stadium, maybe even onto the arena itself. We were wrong. Names were required on pre-printed lists before access was allowed. We climbed a spiked fence successfully, landing on an enclosed bowling-green area, and managed to infiltrate a tourist group entering the Gallery of Sport. It wasn't long before we were sitting in the seats we would occupy the next day. A lone roadie, arse-crack visible even from high in the Southern Stand, sound-checked the microphone on the presentation podium in the centre square. A groundsman wheeled his lime barrow around the huge oval, marking the boundary line and whistling a vaguely familiar tune. The eerie vastness of the surroundings gave little hint of what was to come. We sat without speaking for almost an hour, dreaming of how we might feel if St Kilda won the flag. The silence, as they say, was golden. We were lost in visions of victory. There were butterflies in my stomach. I looked across at Simon and saw goosebumps on his arms.

Winding our way out of the ground, we decided upon a pilgrimage to Trevor Barker's final resting place. We walked from the train station to the New Cheltenham Cemetery, where his cremated remains rested. Stretched out on the grass in the fading light, we cracked a few cans and shared our most cherished Barker memories. We weren't sad or solemn as we spoke of our patron Saint. We were simply paying him our respects on the eve of an event he'd have enjoyed. It felt strange to have outlived him. The notion of his clock stopping reminded me that my own time is ticking away.

Grand Final Day

The MCG carpark was like a reunion. Barbies out of car boots were combined with faces from behind the goals at

Moorabbin. Some had been gone so long, we'd forgotten they were ever there. People who'd worked out that there were other aspects of life worth investigating had come back to collect their chips. Others had gone for reasons they didn't want to discuss. Whatever the circumstances of their absence, they'd returned now. The fun and frivolity took a back seat, however, when it came time to chuck the burnt snags in the rubbish bin and head into the ground for the game. The moment of truth was around the corner, and suddenly I was overcome by a sense of foreboding. Walking up the same stairs as we'd done the day before, I felt physically ill. The majority of St Kilda's supporters had been shepherded by organisers into the same area, high up in the Southern Stand. The sun was shining, but we were seated in shadow. During the pre-game festivities, we took photos of everything and everybody. Whereas the carpark had been buzzing with anticipation only half an hour earlier, an eerie silence now enveloped us. It felt like the total eclipse I'd experienced as a kid which made the local animals go berserk as it was beginning, dogs barking, birds screeching, before settling into a ominous, eye of the storm kind of complete and utter quiet.

Nobody had much to say. There was an encouraging nod here, a firm slap on the shoulder there, but each of us spent a moment alone now with our doubts. Fear crept into our eyes. With the first bounce five minutes away, something had dawned on us all at once. Now, all those long term St Kilda supporters — huddled together in the

Southern Stand, scattered around other parts of the MCG, watching at home, listening on the radio or following on the Internet — suddenly wondered what it might feel like to lose.

We'd never known fear of this sort before. Five wins in a season was a good year for us, not so long ago. We'd been programmed into thinking we had nothing to lose. Now we did, and we weren't used to it. We realised that being beaten would plunge us into emotional waters we had never swum before. As much as St Kilda fans were renowned by opposition players, coaches and supporters for our unequalled passion, as much as they struggled to comprehend the unbridled pleasure we took in an occasional victory during the bad times, so they would struggle to comprehend how hard we'd feel this loss, if it came. If we should fail to grab this chance, today, this afternoon, then that might be *it.* This might be the only chance we have in our lifetime to win The Big One.

While Harvey, Loewe, Burke and Winmar had been and were continuing to be our backbone, our quartet of champions, the main reason for our emergence as a genuine force, they were all getting older and were in the final quarters of their careers. Add to the equation the evenness of the current-day competition, due to salary caps and the draft, and our fear of failure was suddenly all-encompassing. I can't recall attending a single game where I presumed St Kilda *would* win. However, for a variety of reasons — the media making us favourites, the whole of Victoria supporting us against the interstate rivals, Adelaide, and the general popularity of a fairytale finish — now we felt we *should* win.

It was chic to be known as a long-term St Kilda supporter in the week leading up to the game. Simon and I received letters and phone calls from friends and family, wishing us luck. Greg Swedosh and I were almost celebrities in our neighbourhoods for being so committed as to fly around the world 'just for a game of footy!'. St Kilda winning the flag, or the Victorian public's perception of it, represented much more than a game of footy. It was viewed as an example of 'justice for all', 'have faith and you will be rewarded'. The idea of St Kilda winning the flag was like evidence that every dog has its day. If St Kilda could win the premiership, there was hope for us all.

The Aftermath

We lost.

I remember little Aussie Jones and big Barry Hall. That is all.

Our fears were confirmed. For the first time since I began supporting the Saints, I walked out before the end of a game. While I wasn't happy with the players who'd denied me my dream, they weren't the reason for my early departure. No, I left because I'd not flown more than 10,000 miles to hear the fucking Adelaide Crows theme song played repeatedly.

I'd downed six pots in the Cricketers' Arms before the lap of honour was over. Simon stayed, for some reason I still don't respect. By the time he turned up, I'd had ten, but Simon caught up fast. I still haven't watched the game on videotape, and I doubt I ever will. The Cricketers' Arms shut up shop, so we went reeling into the city to continue drowning our sorrows. We were thrown out of one establishment for abusing a barman as he tore down the red, white and black banners from the walls. It wasn't so chic now to be a St Kilda supporter. We'd been pleased with everyone jumping on our bandwagon before the game. We knew where we stood and that they were simply taking sides. It was either us or a side from interstate. Plus, we were just one step away from a rags-to-riches romance. As that barman pulled down the decorations, we knew that while he would've felt great if we'd won, he didn't really care that we hadn't. We, on the other hand, had to suffer the pain.

As I write this, I feel as I felt then.

Like Colonel Walter E. Kurtz, as played by Marlon Brando in Francis Ford Coppolla's *Apocalypse Now*.

Kurtz had entered the Cambodian jungle on a military assignment. Deep into the heart of darkness. He'd reached his breaking point. He was a man who's methods had become unsound. As evidence of his insanity, the authorities played an audio tape of his voice:

'What did you expect?' said Kurtz. 'I supported St Kilda for twenty seasons straight!'

CHAPTER TWENTY-EIGHT

The Back-Track: Trevor Barker Retires

In 1989, upon Trevor Barker's official retirement, St Kilda organised a testimonial night. Arranged in the standard style of a sportsman's night, where selected stars repeat sordid and unprintable tales to an eager all-male audience, the evening was a huge success. Neil and Michael Roberts, Cowboy Neale and Molly Meldrum were among the panel of colleagues and friends offering stories of team trips away, dressing-room debauchery and other such shenanigans. The more booze that was forced back, the funnier each speaker became. This continued until the ex-players were too pissed to proceed. Then the auction began. I decided to bid up to a thousand bucks for Barker's framed jumper. At four hundred, it was between two of us. Drunken blokes began to barrack.

I'd been left a sum of money that became legally mine when I turned eighteen. I ignored my parents' urging to sign it away until I was twenty-one, instead collecting the cash and going on to waste the lot. All I had to show for it when the money ran out was a battered old sharkskin-coloured EH Holden and an increased capacity for drinking beer. I may have also had Trevor Barker's Saints jumper, had it not been for the intervention of Simon, who held my hand down as the bid passed a grand. 'Have you got shit for brains?' he queried in none-too-subtle terms. I think it was Molly Meldrum, a long term contributor to St Kilda's coffers, who finally walked away with the prize possession. A deserving recipient.

As the evening neared its end, with the speeches having ceased and the karaoke underway, I wound my way towards the toilets for a wee. As I stood alone at the trough, full of beer and smiling to myself, who should stagger in and stand to my right but The Great Man himself. Trevor Barker. What an opportunity to pay my respects. I pondered whether to let him piss in peace, but decided to seize the day. 'I doubt you'd remember me, but ...', I began cautiously. 'Matthew! How are ya mate?' he interrupted. No word of a lie, he knew my name. All the contrived excuses I'd invented over the years to approach him in person had paid off. The get-well cards, the witches-hat assistance, the autographs on all kinds of objects had somehow had an impact. Did he know the names of every idiotic idoliser or was I the supreme stalker, the most annoying of all the arseholes? Should I feel pride or shame? I looked him in the eyes and knew at once: he didn't mind. He knew I meant no harm.

'Seriously,' I slurred, 'I wanna thank you for all the pleasure you provided me and my brother. Some of those spekkies were sensayy-shunall'.

'No worries. It's nice of you to say so', he replied, glassy-eyed, suddenly holding himself with his left hand so he could offer me his right. I did the same swap myself and we shook. My dick in one hand, my hero in the other. The moment ended abruptly when Neil Roberts ran in, much the worse for wear, and farted as he executed a chest-high kung-fu kick in Barker's direction. 'Vince', said Trevor as he stumbled back into the bar. I was amazed. We shared more than a love for St Kilda. 'Cattogio', I whispered, following misty-eyed in his footsteps.

CHAPTER TWENTY-NINE

The Final Siren II

What's in store? For the Saints and the whole show. Society today is a more ruthless environment than it once was. In the money-spinning world of first-grade footy, long periods of poor performance are no longer tolerated. Two consecutive seasons without success may see any side facing extinction. Like putting down a pet that's in poor health, the underdogs might end up at the undertakers.

Let us not forget that football is art. People can see a great goal or a particular piece of play they admire and watch it over and over on video. Just as they would listen to a favourite piecelassic of cal music on their sound system. When moving a Picasso from one gallery to another, the utmost care is taken to ensure its safety and preserve the work's original condition. So it should be with our code of football. Nobody expects the game, like the Picasso, to remain in the same place for eternity. View it from a different angle for sure, just don't fuck with what made the art so initially appealing. More important than the moves made around our great game by the men in charge, is the feeling behind each ebb and flow. We have something special here and we mustn't let it slip through out fingers. Change the grip if need be, but never let go. Footy is forever and so are the emotions it inspires.

I'm not sure I enjoy the idea of where we are heading. Plastic seats and mini-pizzas. Light beer and ads on the stars arses. No smoking in the open air. It may all be safer and less expensive but will The Peanut Man and his kind have a place in the grand plan? Where do you unload a gutfull of grog when there are no opening windows on today's trains? Not only is it impossible to buy a hot jam doughnut while watching Fitzroy at the Junction Oval anymore, but it's impossible to watch Fitzroy anywhere at all. What are blokes like Bert Newton going to tell their grandkids? 'Once upon a time' won't be the beginning of a fairy tale. It'll be the start of a ghost story.

Maybe I should shut my mouth. Maybe the men in charge know more about progress than I do. Attendances are at an all-time high. Players are able to earn a living from the game alone. Crowds can watch an instant-replay whenever there's an iffy free-kick. Statistics say that all is well.

Outside the grounds the freeways have become carparks and everything's privatised. Is footy merely following the example set by major corporations across the country? Sure, I'll help roll out the red carpet for every new team the AFL introduces. I wonder if they'll return the favour when *my* side needs assistance? I've loved my team for many moons. I've contributed cash. I've shown support. Now I want some loyalty in return. Today's football generates genuine excitement but I fear what the future holds. I long for the age of innocence. Deep down, part of me will always be sitting in my 'jarmies watching *World of Sport* in front of the fire.

I don't know who makes them now but I might go out and buy a packet of footy cards. See if I can re-create that original adrenaline rush.

End Note

Footy to me is as much about hope, passion and loyalty as it is about pure entertainment. For two hours a week, footy provides the same escapism that I get from watching a Spiderman movie, or seeing AC/DC do a stadium show, or reading a novel on a rainy Sunday morning in the sack. Well, perhaps it provides more than that – it certainly takes me to another place. I forget about the work or the relationships or the bills which otherwise might be causing me concern. Of course, a large part of such escapism is to later share the cultural impact you've experienced personally with others around you. You'll ask a friend if they've seen the movie, if they've heard of the band, if they've read the book. Did they like it? If not, why not? Your opinion will then be either confirmed or placed in doubt under the weight of a varying viewpoint. You might like someone more or less depending on what they think of a certain creative endeavour. 'Really? You liked *Troy*!?! Is that the time, I really should be going.' Or, 'Really? You liked *Kill Bill*!?! So did I, what are you drinking?' The point is, creativity can have a cultural impact, which creates discussion, which encourages community, which helps us learn about ourselves. As can footy and your impression of people depending on who they barrack for or what they thought of a particular game.

Imagine living in a country where music didn't exist. Where if you asked someone whether they'd heard the latest song by, say, Britney Spears, they'd respond by asking what was a song. What about a country where movies didn't exist? Or books? A country where the term 'Lord Of The Rings' elicited no response whatsoever. No, they hadn't seen the movie – mainly because they didn't know what a movie was. Nor had they read the book. They didn't even know what the word 'book' meant. 'You're trying to tell me there's thousands of words printed on hundreds of pages which are arranged in a certain order, so that when you look at them a story unfolds in your mind?' they'd say. 'Get off the grass!' This is pretty much how I'd describe being an AFL follower in England, where I lived and worked through much of the nineties. The English do not know about footy. They do not care. It may as well not exist. The number one interest in my life was eliminated upon arrival.

Try discussing AFL footy with an Englishman. Chances are, if he's seen the game at all, he'll remember the tight shorts and the sleeveless jerseys. At best. He'll probably ask if it's some Aussie version of WWF Wrestling. My English girlfriend, who I lived with in London for three years, who was into sport and who saw me seated before countless video tapes featuring AFL sent from home made one memorable inquiry into the content of what I was watching. 'What's that butcher doing between the big white sticks?' she asked. We split up not long after that.

How do you expect someone to understand why you're supposed to hate Collingwood when they don't know what, who or where a 'Collingwood' is? One bloke I met in Oxford said he thought a 'Barassi' was what we called a really good punch. I'm serious. Unfortunately, so was he. I should've given him a Rhys-Jones for his trouble.

Of course, whenever I went out of my way to try and watch or talk footy at an Aussie-themed pub in England, I'd usually end up drinking with some bloke from Queensland who'd be more into footy than the English, yet more into rugby than Aussie Rules, and so we'd both end up even more homesick than we were before we separately set out to desperately try to find a sporting soul mate from home. And I don't know about him, but after such evenings on the Fosters or the XXXX (which I'd never touch back here, but that's what they think we all drink), I'd then hit the phone and talk to anyone in Australia who'd listen to my drunken, tearful dribble about Brereton at the MCG in the '89 Grand Final, or Micky Conlan in '86 out at Waverley, and the next day the world would be a better place. Until the phone bill arrived the next week.

If absence makes the heart grow fonder then it also makes for a book that has, so far, luckily for me, been well received. It charts my life – one which I feel lucky to have led – from the age of nine through to twenty-nine. From 1979 to 1999. A book which, when I was writing it in London, made me stop for weeks at a time and wonder, why the hell will anyone want to read about my stock-standard suburban existence? A book which has, since hitting the bookshop shelves, seen people I've never met write letters from the strangest places telling me that they thought they were reading their own diary. A woman told me she used to hate footy for stealing the men from her life, but now she understands exactly why her father, brothers, husband and sons have had to heed the call. An e-mail from a fella who'd been working in Zurich for over five years explained how his mum sent a copy after he spoke of being homesick, and reading it had helped. A New Yorker whose visiting Aussie cousin left it behind wrote that he'd read it for something to do one day and was now planning to travel to Australia as a result. A lady said she read it and laughed a lot, but every time she laughed she also cried because she couldn't help but think of her late husband. A man from Sydney, holidaying in Miami, accidentally dropped it off a yacht he was sunning himself on and wanted to know where he could buy another one. I said I'd send a copy over if he could get me Don Johnson's autograph but I haven't heard from him since.

Obviously I'm rapt about these reactions. I'm rapt the book was ever published in the first place. I'm rapt a single copy was ever sold. I'm rapt it sold out the first and second prints at HarperCollins, and I'm rapt it's now been recruited by Jane Palfreyman at Random House. Thank you.

Fortunately, I've been back home a few years now, living again in a country where footy not only exists, but in some ways explains the meaning of life. Well, it does if your team's winning, anyway! Otherwise, 'No way, it was my shout last time!' can be as deep as a day at the footy ever delves. Which is often explanation enough.

At the time of writing, St Kilda – the AFL footy club my life seems to have mirrored – has won the first ten games of the season and are on top of the ladder. An all-time record success rate. It's been a rollercoaster ride up until this point, yet, if the Saints can continue to progress, then hopefully so can I.

trevor barker
FOUNDATION

Trevor Barker was an inspiring player for St Kilda Football Club for over 14 seasons, three of which he was captain. He always provided hope, gave strength and offered inspiration to so many people in need. Sadly, Trevor passed away from cancer in April 1996.

The Trevor Barker Foundation was established in September 1996 to continue the memory and inspirational work of a remarkable man. The Foundation was established by the Crux Club, a non-profit group of sporting, media and business people, in association with Challenge (a cancer support network), and is supported by St Kilda Football Club. Children and their families living with cancer or other life threatening blood disorders are offered support through the Trevor Barker Foundation.

How you can help...

You can help continue Trevor's dreams and memories and support kids with cancer by making a donation to the Trevor Barker Foundation.
Cheques, money orders or credit card details can be sent to the following address:

TREVOR BARKER FOUNDATION
PO BOX 528
TORQUAY VICTORIA 3228
www.trevor-barker-foundation.org

All donations over $2 are fully tax deductible.

My brother's kids are being raised in the same suburban surrounds as we were and I hope they'll one day look back on their childhood with the same affection, where a fight on the lawn with the hose when it's hot is heaven on earth. Sure, I failed to become a footy star, but as their uncle – if I've got anything to impart – it might be that taking your eye off the ball isn't always a bad thing. Sometimes, looking away lets you see some other exciting stuff instead . . .

Matthew Hardy
June 2004